Joseph L. Thomas

Sept. 17, 2006

Grandma Survived
The Titanic

Written by
Joseph L. Thomas

As told by
Anna Thomas

AuthorHouse™
1663 Liberty Drive, Suite 200
Bloomington, IN 47403
www.authorhouse.com
Phone: 1-800-839-8640

AuthorHouse™ UK Ltd.
500 Avebury Boulevard
Central Milton Keynes, MK9 2BE
www.authorhouse.co.uk
Phone: 08001974150

First published by AuthorHouse 3/27/06

ISBN: 1-4259-2192-2 (sc)
ISBN: 1-4259-2191-4 (dj)

Library of Congress Control Number: 2006902562

Printed in the United States of America
Bloomington, Indiana

This book is printed on acid-free paper.

First printing 2002
Second printing 2006

This book is dedicated to my Grandmother, Anna Thomas. This is her story which she told to me many times and which depicts courage of great magnitude.

Table of Contents

About The Author . . .

Born on September 11, 1928, to George and Rose Thomas in Flint, Michigan, I can honestly say I have lived a long and happy life thus far. If I were to live my life over again I wouldn't change a thing. Every phase of my life has been happy and interesting. After graduating High School, I attended Business College and graduated one year later in 1948. To avoid the peace-time draft, I joined the Marine Corps and served faithfully for four years.

After being discharged in 1952, I hired in at Fisher Body Division of the General Motors Corporation. Seven years later, I met and married my lovely wife, Phyllis. We adopted four children, two boys and two girls, plus my Grandmother who lived with us, too. She lived with us for fourteen years before passing away in 1976 at the age of ninety-one. Those years were memorable as she told us her story on many occasions of how she survived the Titanic. Later, as time rolled by, our children blessed us with seven grandchildren, of which two grand-daughters reside in Arizona and one grand-daughter, along with four grandsons, living in Michigan.

I retired from General Motors in 1978 and moved to Arizona in 1981. Lately we have been living six months in Arizona and six months in Michigan.

It was the year 2001 when I decided to write a story about my Grandmother in her honor.

Joseph L. Thomas

i

PREFACE

A choice had to be made quickly, and on the basis of very little information, the officers said the Titanic had struck an iceberg. The extent of the damage was unknown, and at first, not believed to be serious. As a precaution, passengers were asked to put on life jackets. Also, as a precaution, women and children were asked to climb into lifeboats, to be rowed a safe distance from the ship until the emergency had passed. Slowly, one by one, the Titanic lifeboats were rowed silently into the void, to a distance where the survivors huddled in them could see the whole length of the ship, like the skyline of a city tilting crazily into the water.

A DEBT OF GRATITUDE

As a tribute to Anna Thomas and her two children who survived the sinking of the Titanic, I would like to personally thank Mr. James Cameron for his achievement in the production of the Titanic film. It was as close to reality as my grandmother, Anna Thomas, had related it to me so many times.

The two children were George, age 8, and Mary, age 12. George was my father.

FORWARD

Most of us are not old enough to remember the sinking of the Titanic, since most of us were not even born, but almost everyone has a vivid, mental picture of the last minutes in the life of the huge, luxurious liner that was supposed to be unsinkable. We can see the great ship, ablaze with lights and tilting severely by the bow as the lifeboats were slowly moving away. We can only imagine what it must have been like to sit in one of those small boats and look back, or stand on the slanting deck when the realization that the unsinkable ship was going down, must have struck even the most faithful. The "women and children" mandate, though it was not followed to the letter, is an integral part of the legend, and the cause of more than one childhood nightmare, in which husbands and fathers were forever lost beneath the icy black water.

Since it sank on April 14, 1912, the Titanic has been the subject of an endless stress of books, pamphlets, magazine articles, films, and even in the 1930s a country song was written by Roy Acuff, "What a Shame, When That Gre-e-eat Ship Went Down."

It has been 90 years since the sinking of the Titanic, but the story, as told by Anna Thomas, is as compelling and popular as any ever written.

PROLOGUE

During the early years of Grandma Anna's life in Lebanon and before she married Darwin Toma, it was a tradition that the siblings of the family acquired their father's first name as their last name. In this case my grandmother's father's name was Joseph Rassey or Yousef Rassey. Therefore grand-mother's maiden name was Anna Yousef until she married Darwin Toma. When grandma Anna purchased the ship fare she had inadvertently given her name as Anna Yousef and the children as Maria Yousef and George Yousef. In the United States, it was the Toma family as shown on the birth certificates of her three Sons who were born after she arrived in America. 'Later when my father went into the grocery business, he changed the family name to Thomas.

My father George Thomas (Yousef) attended the 1982 Convention of the Titanic Historical Society in Philadelphia along with Frank Aks, Edwina MacKenzie, Eva Hart, Ruth Blanchard, Walter Lord and many others who attended. He also attended the 1987 Convention of the Historical Society in Wilmington, Delaware

He was also interviewed by Joan Lundon on the *Good Morning America* show the next day. My father appeared on many talk shows, television, and had a huge article in the *Parade Magazine* of the Detroit Newspaper. Each year on the anniversary of the sinking of the Titanic, my father would be interviewed by local newspapers in Michigan and Phoenix, Arizona, and also live coverage on radio in both places.

In April of 1998, I was interviewed in Arizona by the *Mesa Tribune* newspaper. This large article was in behalf of grandma

1

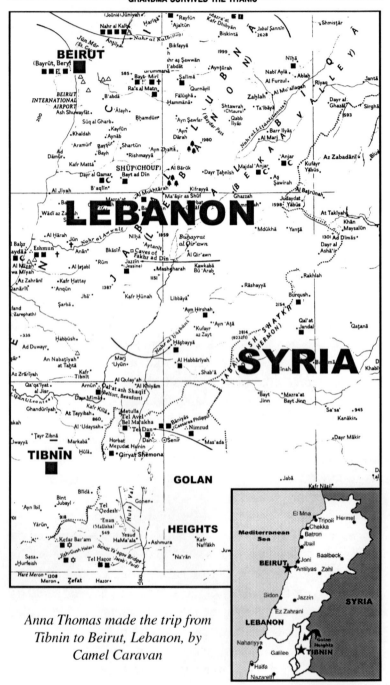

*Anna Thomas made the trip from
Tibnin to Beirut, Lebanon, by
Camel Caravan*

2

Anna, who was never interviewed about the Titanic. In fact, the stories of the Titanic surfaced after grandma's death and every year thereafter. This book is in her memory, of her courage and her love for us and my love for her.

In 1961, just two years after Phyllis and I were married, Grandma Anna asked if she could live with us. She was seventy-six years old. Those fifteen years that she lived with us were the years that she really spoke about her terrifying experience on the Titanic, a ship that was advertised as *unsinkable*. Grandma didn't know this, of course. To her it was a big boat that would take her to America after her days of traveling from a little village of Tibnin in Lebanon.

Her husband, Darwin, had saved a little money to pay for his passage to America, money he saved working in onion fields. His brother, Abraham, went with him. Their plan, as most immigrants strived for, was to earn enough to send for their families. For Darwin it was to send for his wife and two children. He had no success in this and seven years passed. Still there was not enough money for Anna and her children to join him. How could he save when he had been sending her a little money from time to time so there was not much left for saving?

Abraham, on the other hand, had saved enough since he had no one to send money to in Lebanon. He knew how sad his brother was and how much he missed his family so since he had saved enough money he would use some of it for Anna's passage. It was to be a surprise for Darwin so he sent for his wife Anna and their children. He sent Anna a piece of paper along with enough money for the trip which said, "Dowagiac, Michigan, U.S.A." He was going to surprise his brother Darwin.

Anna treasured this piece of paper. It was where her husband lived, even though she had no idea where this place was. The paper said Dowagiac, Michigan, U.S.A., and that's where she was going.

During all of the years that Grandma lived with us, my wife and I asked her many questions about her trip to America. We also asked her about her age when she married Darwin along with his age. She said that in Lebanon in those days no one had birth certificates. Age was mandated by the seasons of the year. Grandma said she was born fifteen seasons before the turn of the Century, which placed her birth about 1885. Darwin was born about 30 seasons before the turn of the Century, which placed his birth about 1870.

She said they were married about one season before the turn of the Century, which placed the date at 1899. She said that when a woman reached the age of puberty, she was ready for marriage. She was fourteen and Darwin was twenty-nine.

Darwin's aunt lived with them until she passed away sometime between the time Darwin left for America and the time Anna left for America. I asked Grandma the ages of her children, Maria, my Aunt, and George, my father. She thought about it for a few minutes then said Maria was born right at the turn of the Century and George about four seasons later. Therefore, at the time they left for America, Anna was twenty-seven, Maria twelve and George was eight.

I asked her how she survived in Lebanon and she said Darwin worked the onion field and for other farmers in that area. He had enough money saved up for his trip to America. Anna worked the farm while Darwin was gone and saved what she could. Darwin's aunt had some money which was left her when her husband passed away.

After seven long years Anna received a letter from her beloved husband Darwin with money for her and the children to come to America. Abraham had made it look like Darwin had sent her the money. She wasted little time selling her personal items and the hut she lived in.

I asked her if she enjoyed her trip to Beirut by camel caravan. She replied the days were long and exhausting and the nights short. Not enough sleep to rest up. The caravan company supplied the tents to sleep in and the food which they ate. It consisted of yogurt cheese and olives stuffed in Arabic pocket bread, spiced with onions and garlic; they washed it down with homemade wine. This was always a favorite meal among the Arabs. Grandma Anna was Christian, but many Arabs were Muslims. She had tears in her eyes when she mentioned that there were a dozen families from her tiny village that accompanied them on this trip to America and who drowned on the Titanic since they were locked in steerage. These were memories that were locked in her heart and spilled out many times when she spoke about her ordeal when the Titanic sank and shocked the world.

The tears were wiped and she smiled as she related how enjoyable the evenings were as the villagers had brought their own musical instruments with them. They had homemade flutes made from hollow pipes with holes in them and small hand drums covered with goat skins. The majestical flutes played several Arabic songs to the beat of the drums. Everyone danced in a circle with the men spinning their handkerchiefs high into the air. Even Maria and George enjoyed dancing along with a few other children as they tried to keep up with the adults. The Arabic dance was called the "Dub—Ke."

When Grandma reached Beirut, she left the camel caravan and followed those going to America to a freighter. I asked her how she enjoyed her trip on the freighter from Beirut to France. She said that the food was lousy and the cabin was very small compared to the Titanic. However, they enjoyed the boat ride to France which took five days.

"We, and all those of us from my village boarded a train in France," Grandma said, "and the children ran through all of the cars to see if there were any other children on the train besides the ones traveling with the villagers."

Maria and George told their mother that the other children on the train spoke very differently and they could not understand them. However, they found a way to amuse themselves for three days on the train to Cherbourg. I asked Grandma Anna if she had to wait very long in Cherbourg for the Titanic to arrive. She replied, "Yes, we waited for about six days and (we) were placed in a nice hotel with the rest of the villagers."

Then I asked her about her ordeal aboard the Titanic and she told my wife and I the complete story. My wife couldn't bear to hear the entire story and departed to our bedroom and began to cry. Grandma did the same thing. As she was telling the story she would stop and cry for a few minutes, then continue.

She didn't like the children to wonder all over the Titanic, which they did. On that night of April 14th, George was in their cabin, but Maria had not returned. This worried her. She stood in the doorway of her cabin talking to one of the travelers from her village when the Titanic hit the iceberg. She didn't know it was an iceberg; it was just a jolt at the time. The jolt made her door slam shut cutting her hand along the index finger. Two of the village men were sent to find out what had happened while Grandma went to the infirmary to get her hand bandaged. She noticed that everyone she passed was wondering why the engines had stopped and what the jolt was. The people looked serious but she could not understand them. The village men returned and said the ship had struck an iceberg. They were instructed to stay calm in their cabins and pray.

"They want me to pray," said Grandma. "That I will do but I better find out what I have to pray about." She took George by the hand and headed for the top deck. They were boosted up from deck to deck by the crew members. When they reached the top where the lifeboats were, Grandma proved she was no dummy. She saw people dressed in furs and beautiful clothes. The men were dressed for evening and music was being played. No one seemed to take it seriously, but when Grandma saw these beautifully dressed people getting

6

into the little boats and complaining, she knew that was the place to go. She instructed George to stay put. She had to return for Maria and her precious piece of paper stating where her husband lived.

She arrived back at the cabin in time to see Maria come out of the cabin next door where she had been napping. "Maria," she yelled, quick get dressed! George is way up on the top deck; we must run as fast as we can because he is all alone up there." She quickly helped Maria into her coat, grabbed her money and that precious slip of paper, and raced, with Maria, down the passage way that lead out of steerage. As they left the steerage area she heard a loud bang. Looking back she saw the steerage section's gate had been closed and was being locked. She thought it was for safety of some kind and did not bother to think about it much as she headed for the top deck. They were climbing up from deck to deck, stopping only to grab three life jackets. They found George just where she had left him. He related in tears how some of the people wanted to put him in the boats but he would not go without his mama. A nice man with a beard helped them into Lifeboat Two. There were twenty-five people in that boat which could have held many more.

The descent was terrifying. The water was seventy feet below and the sailors let out the rope a little at a time causing the boat to rock and sway. Grandma prayed. The children wanted to know what happened to the big boat and what were they doing in the small boat. Grandma said the big boat had something wrong with it and that's why they were in the small boat.

Grandma covered George and Maria with her cloak so they would not see the big ship break and sink. She cried for her fellow villagers. She watched people jump into the water off the boat. Screams, then silence. It was freezing cold, and the view was something Grandma could never forget. The enormity of the ship looked unreal. A sixth of a mile long, seventy-five feet high up to the top deck, with hundreds of portholes all lit up and slowly being extinguished one by one. The cries of people in the water soon stopped and it became very quiet.

The sky was black with millions of stars all the way in the distance where the sky and waterline became one. It was so black you could not see who else was in the boat. They were all in a state of shock.

When dawn broke, they saw a ship in the distance. God had given them a miracle. Grandma's boat was the second to be rescued by the *Carpathia*. George was placed in a sack and pulled up on deck. He was the first to set foot on the boat.

Headlines of the sinking of the Titanic were big news. In Dowagiac, Michigan, Abraham was shocked at the news and felt guilty because he believed he was the cause of his brother, Darwin, losing his family. How was he to tell him that they were on the Titanic and now were gone? But tell him he did— Darwin nearly went crazy. He chased him up and down the street. If he had caught him would have beat the hell out of him. They both cried in sadness and rage, both devastated.

Five days later they received a cable from a priest who spoke Arabic. He had a message for someone in Dowagiac. His wife and children had been saved. Fifty-six days after leaving her little village in Lebanon, Grandma, George and Maria arrived in Dowagiac. That little piece of paper with Dowagiac, Michigan, had found her husband for her.

Grandma would have loved the movie TITANIC. I loved it and now know what Grandma meant when she said the big boat broke and sank. When I saw the movie it actually did break before sinking. It was as close to reality as Grandma had related to me so many times.

GROWING UP WITH GRANDMA

I was born on September 11, 1928, in a large two story home in flint, Michigan, along with my father George (the boy of eight who had survived the Titanic) and mother Rose and sister Emily. The home was also occupied by Grandma Anna, Grandpa Darwin, and my three uncles, Samuel, age fifteen, Francis, age fourteen, and Joseph W., age twelve. Grandma had three more children over the years, and we all lived in the same house.

My Uncle Sam helped my father in the grocery business on a full time basis, while my uncles, Francis and Joe, were still in school. My grandfather Darwin also helped my father at the store along with other chores that Grandma Anna might designate around the house. During the weekends, Francis and Joe would help at the store. My mother helped Grandma Anna with the housework chores such as cooking, washing and ironing, dusting, and so forth.

My mother developed into a fantastic cook as she learned it all from the greatest cook, Grandma Anna. Cooking has been a tradition in our family as it has been handed down from one generation to another and, to this day in the year 2001, my sisters and I consider ourselves *Chefs in Arabic Cuisine'*.

My father had previously purchased the store from his uncle, Elias Rassey, who taught him the business in 1927. Elias was Grandma Anna's brother.

Uncle Rassey was a Christian Warrior in his younger days in Lebanon. He fought against the Muslims for control of the country. He left Lebanon after Grandma Anna and established himself in the grocery business in Flint, Michigan, in the early 1920s.

Grandma Anna's brother Elias Rassey had a son and two daughters. His son, Joseph Rassey, passed away in the 1940s at a young age in his twenties. His daughters, Mary and Lieyah Rassey, married the Zerka cousins, Sam and Jack. Between them they had many beautiful children. Elias Rassey and the Zerka cousins became partners in the grocery business and opened a few stores in Flint, Michigan, called "Zerka & Rassey Supermarkets."

Grandma Anna also had a sister (the youngest of the family) who flew in from France to visit Grandma and the family in the 40s. I will never forget the first time I saw her—she looked exactly like Grandma Anna—she even acted like her. They would talk for hours about their younger days when they were in Lebanon and laughed at the things they had done in their younger days.

Business was great for the next two years as my father established a host of credit customers. Then it happened! On October 24, 1929, the Stock market crashed. Those who well remembered that day, called it Black Thursday. My father had his profits deposited in a local bank which folded almost immediately. Many of my father's credit customers were also unable to fulfill their obligations. Eventually, the bank fulfilled their obligations, but it took them ten years to do it.

Grandma Anna helped during the crisis by asking Grandpa Darwin to bring home from the store any partially spoiled fruits and vegetables. She would remove the spoiled spots and use the good parts. She made apple pie and apple sauce almost every day, and we all had plenty of salad to eat.

Living in the same house with Grandma Anna was like living with another mother. She would rock me to sleep as my mother always did along with an abundance of hugs and kisses. I presume that I was spoiled at an early age. In fact, it only got worse as I grew older.

I loved my Grandmother very dearly and she always protected me and stood-up for me during my adolescent years. I was reminded of one incident that happened when I was about three years old. My grandmother's devotion to me was so incredible on this one particular day, that her response to my actions will be remembered forever. A thundering crash in the living room startled Grandpa Darwin, who was sound asleep in his chair in another room, and Grandma Anna, who was cooking supper in the kitchen. They both ran toward me as I was laying on the floor with a broken lamp resting beside me. Grandpa and Grandma simultaneously screamed, "Are you OK.?—Are you hurt?—What happened?"

I looked up at them with a very innocent expression on my face and said, "I didn't do it, I didn't push the lamp off the table. It was Emily that did it and she ran upstairs to hide."

My grandparents looked at each other and roared with laughter as tears streamed down their cheeks. They picked me up and hugged and kissed me and said, "We will have a little talk with Emily later."

This episode was the topic of tremendous laughter by the entire family at the dinner table. I laughed with them, however, I never knew until much later in time that Emily was very sick and in the hospital with pneumonia and that I was the only child in the house.

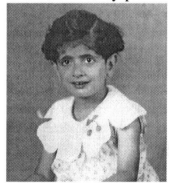

*Sister Betty at age three
in 1936*

Grandma Anna spent many nights with Emily at the hospital as she and my mother took turns looking after her. Emily was never left alone and she had many visitors.

My younger sister, Beatrice, was born in May of 1933. It was her turn to be spoiled as Emily and I had been. In September of the same year, I became five years old and was very adamant about going to school. With Emily and my friends at school, I didn't want to be left alone without anyone to play with. I begged my mother to let me attend school where all of the teachers were Nuns! The Priests were also teachers as well as activity directors. I was enrolled in the first grade as there were no kindergarten classes at that school. I was dressed in knickers which in those days was an ongoing style for boys. They were short trousers, which were gathered just below the knees. They looked an awful lot like grandma's bloomers except that my knickers were brown in color and not white. I had short curly hair and, at first sight, the Nun in my class placed a ribbon on my hair and paraded me through each class in school. All the children laughed at me until I began to cry. I broke away from the Nun and ran home which was one block away and I cried all the way. Grandma Anna caught me at the door and asked, 'Why aren't you at school? Why are you crying?" She examined the ribbon in my hair and asked, "What is this ribbon doing in your hair?" After I explained to her what had happened, she immediately grabbed a broomstick and headed for the school. She was very angry with the Nun for 'embarrassing her grandson and making him cry' and she was going to pop that Nun on the head with her broomstick.

She ran half way to the school when she noticed the Nun running towards her with tears in her eyes. Grandma, quickly waving the stick yelled, "Are you the one who make shame on my grandson and make him cry?"

The Nun replied very shamefully and apologized for the incident. She said,"I had no idea that Joe was so sensitive and I thought that he was enjoying it, too. It will never happen again and I would like to escort him back to school." Grandma and the Nun became good friends after that.

In 1937, when I was eight years old and Emily was ten, we took our first Holy Communion at "All Saints Church."

Joe and Emily at their first Holy Communion, 1937

As you can see I was wearing knickers and still had curly hair. The only ribbon I had at this time was attached to my lapel. Emily looked fascinating in her getup, however, this was the custom dress in those days.

I adored my grandmother as she was always there to protect me from everyone, especially our next door neighbor, Mike. He was a mean old Polish fellow who lived alone in the house next to ours. He had a Plum tree in his back yard and one of the limbs extended into our yard. I would always climb on it and play. Mike didn't like that and told me to get off his tree or else he would pull me off and spank me. My grandfather Darwin heard this and immediately jumped off the back porch and ran to the edge of the fence and told Mike, "You *toucha* my grandson and *I breaka* you face." I won that round as long as I stayed on our side of the fence and didn't climb beyond the limb on our side.

Mike stayed away from the back yard for a few days as he would never tangle with my grandpa. It was always a pleasure to listen to Grandpa and Grandma speak with broken English, however they always got their point across. By spoiling me the way they did, I became more daring and was looking for trouble just to see what their limits would be and to see how far I could go beyond their tolerance.

I was eight years old at that time. The weekends were very lonely without any action and I was tired of playing with the neighborhood kids. One Saturday morning I called my cousin Bill (Aunt Mary's son) and asked him to come over and play. Cousin Bill was the oldest son of Aunt Mary and about a year younger than I. However, he was just a bit taller than me but we always thought alike. In fact, during our escapades, he would get me in trouble and I would get blamed for it. This was the beginning of a brotherly friendship whereby we got into mischief together. If I didn't think of something crazy to do, he certainly would.

One day while we were playing in Mike's plum tree we

noticed that Mike's basement window was open. It was a unanimous decision that we should peg a few plums through the basement window with a grand prize of a slice of Grandma's apple pie for the one who pegged the most plums through the open window. Neither one of us won the prize as Mike was in the basement and he poked his head through the window shaking his fists and cursing us in Polish. "Whata hella you do?" He barked as he tried to climb out of the window. Bill and I almost broke a leg jumping off the limb, and worst of all, Grandpa Darwin was on the porch noticing everything. Realizing this, Bill said, "Joe, I think you won the grand prize and besides, I can hear my mother calling me." And he raced for home as fast as he could go.

He lived about a mile away, but at a time like this he made it home in about five minutes and I was left holding the bag. Grandpa caught me inside the house and gave me a sound thrashing. After the tears dried, Grandma Anna gave me a slice of the grand prize. Then she told me that I was wrong and made me promise not to do that again. Then she grabbed her broom stick and shook it over grandpa's head yelling, "You no *toucha* my Joe again!" Of course she was winking at grandpa all of the time. Then I realized that the limits and tolerance should not be tried again. I sure loved that Grandma Anna of mine.

The next weekend Bill came over and we decided to stay out of the plum tree. Instead we thought it would be great fun to walk barefooted behind the house into the soft dirt that Grandpa Darwin was plowing and cultivating for at least a week. We made a few rounds and began to play tag when, all of a sudden, Grandpa came running out of the house yelling, "*Whata* you do to my *fresha* garden?" At this point Bill ran out through the back gate and down the alley yelling, "Goodbye Joe, my mother is calling me again." I was out the same gate as Grandpa gave chase. As I rounded the far corner, I could see him coming. I ran faster and faster just hoping that

I could go all the way around the block and into the house through the front door. Grandpa Darwin was thinking the same as I was and knowing what I was going to do, he doubled back through the back gate and into the house. As I entered the front door, he was holding a large strap which he used to sharpen his razor. He grabbed me and promised me a sound thrashing again. However, he did not notice that Grandma Anna was behind him waving the broom stick. She told grandpa, "You no *toucha* Joe, he *nota* know you *starta* garden." I was saved again and another piece of apple pie. I just loved that Grandma Anna.

The following weekend, Bill and I were absolutely lost. We just couldn't think of anything exciting to do. Grandma Anna had just pulled a few pies out of the oven and set them on the windowsill to cool. The window was open and the aroma was devastating. We decided that when the pies had cooled off, we would each grab a pie and run into the back garage and eat them.

"We could always blame the neighbor kids for stealing them," Bill said.

"Good idea," I replied.

As we were leaving with the pies, Grandpa Darwin caught us and asked what we intended to do and where we were going with the pies. At this time, Grandma Anna, who was still in the kitchen, heard Grandpa and shouted at him, "I *aska* them to *checka* the pies to *seea* if they cooled down and to *bringa* them into the house when they are ready."

Grandpa Darwin replied, "The pies *are-ah* ready and we are bringing them in." We all sat at the table enjoying the pies when Grandpa Darwin asked cousin' Bill, "Don't you hear your mother calling you?"

"Nope," Bill answered, as he reached for another piece of pie and we all busted out laughing.

In another instance when Bill, came over on Saturday, Grandpa Darwin asked us what mischief we were planning for today. We told him that we would like to see the movie across the street if we had ten cents (each) to get in. We were blessed that there was a movie hall just across the street and on Saturdays they showed cartoons and westerns all afternoon. Grandpa Darwin mentioned that this was the best offer he has had in over a month and told us to watch the movies over and over if we wanted to. We ran into the house to tell Grandma where we were going and she insisted that we take a lunch with us. She packed a large sack with good Arabic food called Kibby and we went to the movies. It was very crowded, but we found a couple of vacant seats in the middle of the theater. After about thirty minutes we started to get hungry and started eating the Kibby which was a special blend of meat, wheat and lots of onions. It took about the length of two cartoons to clear the theater. As we looked around us, we noticed that there was no one around us for at least ten rows in each direction. After the movies were over, we returned home and found the family gathered around the dinner table. When we told them what had happened at the movies, my uncles Sam and Francis laughed so hard they actually fell out of their chairs.

Uncle Francis and Uncle Sam

These sort of things would happen every time Bill came over. In winter we would toss snowballs at anyone or anything that moved or accidentally run over anyone with our sleds.

Another very important time in my life with grandma Anna happened when I was ten years old. I was very sick with a stomach ache for about three days. My Grandmother checked me for fever and upon noticing how hot my forehead was to her warm hands, she let out a scream and called my father at the store. He arrived quickly and bundled me with a warm blanket and carried me to the car. With Grandma Anna at my side, I felt safe and secure. I was rushed to our family doctor, Dr. Goodfellow diagnosed that my appendix had burst and there was little time to spare. The doctor ordered my father to rush me to the emergency room at the hospital while he called a couple of surgeons. Upon arriving at the hospital two highly respected surgeons were waiting for me. After confirming Dr. Goodfellow's diagnosis, I was immediately prepped for surgery and wheeled into the operating room. Needless to say, Grandma Anna was crying very hard and feared the worse. She was directed to the hospital Chapel and prayed and prayed. After several hours, she was escorted by a nurse to the room, which I called my home for five weeks. When she arrived I was unconscious and in a coma. Grandma Anna stayed with me day and night and refused to go home until her prayers were answered. Ten days later I awoke to find Grandma Anna smiling at me as she raised both arms high into the air to praise God. Yes! I will never forget my grandmother. I loved her very much.

After abut three weeks, they allowed my sister Emily to visit me. When she walked into the room and saw me, she began to cry as she had missed me too. I was very happy to see her.

To this day, in the year 2002, Bill and I still talk about the *good old days* and have a good laugh. In fact, it was so much fun that if we had to do it all over again, we wouldn't change a thing.

THE WAR YEARS

This was a devastating time in Anna's life. Uncle Joe, Anna's son, had just finished Medical College as World War II began. It was in 1942 when Joe entered the Army as a doctor and was immediately commissioned. His service will long be remembered as he introduced many lifesaving ideas to the army while he was with the Seventh Indian Head Division. He was highly praised in *Time Magazine* for his unchallenging efforts. Grandma Anna prayed and cried every day while he was overseas.

Uncle Sam and Uncle Francis were busy at the grocery store, which was expanded into a Super Market. My father George sold the store to my Uncles in 1940 and they built the business tremendously. This was the first and largest Super Market in the State of Michigan at that time.

My father purchased a small store in the suburbs in 1940 and I helped him nightly after school and on weekends. I would visit Grandma Anna

Lt. Col. Joseph W. Thomas

every Sunday as she and Grandpa Darwin and my uncles remained in the old house. I would ride my bicycle eight miles every Sunday morning to Grandma's house to see her. She always had breakfast ready for me and once in a while Cousin Bill would be there waiting for me. After breakfast, Bill and I would ride our bikes to church, and then go our separate ways. He would return home and so would I, as my father needed me at the store. He would close the store on Sundays from one P.M. to five P.M. as my father needed plenty of rest. During the week, he opened the store at seven A.M. and closed about ten P.M.

As the war came to an end in 1945, so did the life of Grandpa Darwin, unexpectedly. As he was climbing the stairs to go to bed, he stopped about half way and called for help. My uncles Sam and Francis ran up the stairs and helped him to his room. Dr. Goodfellow was summoned immediately and upon arriving examined Grandpa and then, pronounced him dead. This was a blow to Grandma Anna. I thought she would never stop crying. For the next thirty years, Grandma would shed many tears whenever she talked about Grandpa Darwin.

The following year when Uncle Joe was out of the Army, he and his brothers Sam and Francis decided that the best thing to do was to sell the store and house and relocate to California and start a new life there. Such a move would be good for their mother Anna and the weather would be better for her. She was so lonely for Darwin that everyone thought that moving to California was the right thing to do.

They did just that. They lived in North Hollywood where they immediately got jobs in the large supermarkets, there, all except Joe. He went into private practice, but didn't enjoy the hustle and bustle of traffic in the office. He quit and went back into the Army and was stationed in Texas where he purchased a home and also raised his wonderful family. Grandma didn't mind as long as the war was over and he stayed in the United States. She was, however, lonely for the rest of family in Michigan, so she would return and spend summers in Michigan with her daughter Mary (Maria) and her family. I loved my grandma and missed her very much. It was such a pleasure to see her in the summer time. I finished high school in 1947 and college in 1948. I served four years in the Marine Corps from 1948 to 1952. During this time, the Korean War started and Uncle Joe was sent to a MASH Unit in Korea. Grandma Anna wasn't too happy about that.

GRANDMA ANNA RETURNS TO MICHIGAN

In 1953 Anna's daughter, Maria, was the first of the Titanic survivors of the 'Yousef' family to pass away. She was ill for quite some time and her untimely passing created yet another hardship for Grandma, as she never expected to outlive any of her children. This created a problem for Grandma Anna as she didn't know which way to turn. She would cry a lot and then wish she had never sold her home in Michigan. She always said, "If I still had my home, I could have all of my grandchildren visit me from the Haddad family and the Thomas family. But, that could never be. Grandma Anna could never live alone since her grandchildren had grown. My sister, Emily, invited her to live with her and her husband, Howard in Pontiac, Michigan. She accepted and lived happily with them for about eight or nine years. She visites the rest of the family and they would also come over to see her. Her broken English never changed and it was always so much fun to listen to her. My sister, Emily, had a pet parakeet, which Grandma had a lot of fun talking to. In fact she taught the bird how to wake up Howard on Sunday mornings—the parakeet spoke perfect broken English:

"*Geta offa* the bed, breakfast is *ona* the table.'

"Howard, *ifa* you *noa* get *upa* you breakfast go *outa*."

Yes, Grandma enjoyed her stay with Emily and Howard. With 90% of her family residing in Michigan, Anna really never wanted to go back to California except to visit. With the Korean War over and Uncle Joe assigned to an Army Hospital near his home in Texas, and Sam and Francis in California. Grandma Anna could travel to three different states to

21

see all of her family which made her very happy.

I met my wife Phyllis in the Spring of 1959; we were married in the fall. Cousin Bill had met and married about five years before us. His wife's name is June. When the four of us got together, Bill and I would talk about the good old days and all of our escapades along with it. The four of us would laugh the night away, however, our wives learned a lot about us and what kind of guys they married. Every spring when we got together and talked about the good old days, we recalled the time we went North to go fishing for smelt.

One never used a fishing pole to catch them. We wore hip boots and used a large net. We drove up there on a Friday night after work in my car. We had the boots and net, but we had forgotten to bring buckets to put them in. Bill had a good idea, although I really didn't care for it. He said that we could toss the Smelt in the trunk and hurry home when we were finished. He wouldn't have thought of that if it had been his car. However, it was too late to turn back and the stores were closed. We filled the trunk and hurried home, about one hundred miles, where Bill removed about half of the smelly Smelt from the trunk and said good night. I went on home and removed the rest of the smelly Smelt. At least I thought I had. In the middle of summer, and on the hottest day of the year, while the sun was beating down on my car, a very strong odor emerged from the trunk. I quickly opened it and immediately noticed that I had forgotten a few pieces of Smelt inside the center of my spare tire. They were moldy and full of maggots. I threw the tire out and flushed out the trunk with a hose and left it open to dry in the hot sun, Incidentally, I gave some smelt to Grandma Anna as she always loved fish. When I told her what had happened, she asked me if Bill mentioned his mother calling him after he said good night. We laughed.

MY LIFE WITH PHYLLIS

In 1961 just two years after Phyllis and I were married, Grandma Anna asked if she could live with us. We welcomed her with open arms and she lived out her life with us, about fifteen years.

Those were the memorable years. She told us her story of the journey from Lebanon to Dowagiac, Michigan, and her ordeal on the Titanic many times. It was an experience that had been with her as if it had happened yesterday.

My wife and I adopted four children and Grandma loved them as if they were her own.

During all of these years that Grandma stayed with us, there were many questions that my wife and I would ask her about her trip to America. We heard the same story over and over for many years. I asked her if anyone else heard the story from her and she replied, "Yes, while the children were young and growing up, they enjoyed hearing the same story over and over on cold wintry nights as we huddled together beside the wood burning stove."

Yes, I loved my Grandma Anna very much and I miss her terribly. I always thanked her for her courage because if it weren't for that I would not be alive today to write this book. George, who was eight, is my father. If he had perished when the Titanic went down, I would never have been born. I wouldn't have my cousin Bill and the rest of the Haddad family as well as my sisters, as we all grew up together as a very close family.

Speaking of cousin Bill, he and his lovely wife, June, came to our house to visit Grandma Anna at least once a week. We always talked about the good old days and laughed. Grandma

23

Anna enjoyed talking about the good old days so much that I believe she was living in the past.

There was a time just before Easter Sunday when Bill and I, our wives and Grandma decided to bake some *Arabic Easter* cookies. Grandma told Bill and I what ingredients to purchase from the store. We started out mixing the flour, sugar and butter until it had the correct texture. Grandma would taste the dough and mention there was too much butter or not enough sugar. After returning from the store again, we added the sugar and started mixing again. After tasting it again, she said there was too much sugar and not enough flour. Needless to say, we went back and forth to the store most of the afternoon until we finally had the right texture.

After spending some six hours baking cookies, we ended up splitting about forty dozen each. This, Bill and I would laughed about for many years to come, especially at Easter time.

Another hilarious incident happened in 1945 just after the war ended. The factories were building cars again and everyone was selling off their old one. Cousin Bill bought an old jalopy and one day he drove to grandma Anna's house to show off his car. Grandma was busy in the kitchen, but uncle Francis was in the living room in his pajamas reading the evening paper. It was about ten P.M. when Bill showed up. He asked uncle Francis if he would go for a ride in his car. Francis said, "Sure, but wait until I get dressed and put some shoes on." Bill said, "You won't have to get dressed, just jump into the car and we will ride around the block a couple of times— the car is just in front of the house."

Francis accepted and they both jumped into the car. They were just two blocks from home when the car suddenly stopped. Francis asked, "Why are we stopping?"

Bill said, "That's it!"

Francis hollered, "What do you mean *that's it*?"

Bill said that the motor is hot and it needs to cool off for a couple of hours before it can start up again.

Francis said, "We are stopped in the middle of the road and I am in my pajamas and barefooted." He also said, "If a policeman sees me, I could get arrested for vagrancy."

Bill said, "The only other thing you can do is run home as fast as you can and try not to look conspicuous."

He jumped out of the car and started running as though he was in the Olympics. In fact, he could have received a Gold Medal if he was. He ran between houses, through the alley, and down the street and arrived home in record time. When he arrived inside the house Grandma asked him where he went without his clothes on. When he told her what had happened, she laughed hysterically.

Our children grew up around Grandma Anna and when she would speak to them she spoke in two different languages, half Arabic and half English. When my youngest daughter, Clarene, was three years old, Anna would ask her to get her something in her bedroom and would speak in Arabic in doing so. Clarene would retrieve whatever Anna asked for and understood her completely. As time went on our children grew up understanding the Arabic language, but could not speak it as my wife and I insisted they speak only English as they were taught in school.

Grandma Anna became weaker and weaker as she grew older, and by 1974 her circulation had almost shut down completely. It was decided amongst the family that it would be best if she would live out the rest of her days in a nursing home which was located a mile (or so) from our house. We did not want the children to see grandma Anna as often as they wanted to, but I stopped in to see her everyday on my way home from work and on weekends.

Before she was admitted into the nursing home, she gave me something to remember her by. It was an 1874 Gold British Sovereign, which she had carried with her on the Titanic. The Purser aboard the Titanic gave her the coin as change for her family fare. It was in mint condition. She asked me to keep it as long as possible as it could be worth a lot of money some

25

day. I later took it to a coin dealer and had it encased and labeled. He said that it was 91.7% gold according to the book that he was identifying it with.

All her life, Grandma Anna wanted to be a U.S. Citizen more than anything else in the world. It was a dream come true

Soverign 1874   Great Britain

Full 91.7   Gold

when my father George surprised her at the nursing home. One day he brought a Judge with him from the circuit court to swear her in as a U.S. Citizen. It was a big day for her as there were photographers taking pictures, and news media capturing everything she said on television as well as in the newspaper.

Grandma spent the holidays with us at our home for the festive dinners on Easter, Thanksgiving, and Christmas. Easter of 1976 was the last dinner she had with us at our home as that beautiful grandmother of ours went to heaven on Monday, June 28, 1976.

I shall never forget that day. My wife received a call from the nursing home explaining that we had lost Grandma Anna. After my wife was able to compose herself, she called me at work and broke the news to me. Even though I knew she was failing, the sudden shock took me by surprise and I let out a horrid scream as I broke down and cried like a baby. My co-workers ran to me and between sobs, I told them that I lost one of the bravest women in the world that had ever lived, my Grandma Anna. I loved her so very much. My boss offered to drive me home but after a few minutes, I left by myself.

For a long time I felt unprotected, insecure and depressed, as my childhood days backed up on me. Then my wife took command of the situation and has spoiled me ever since.

Summary of the Survivors

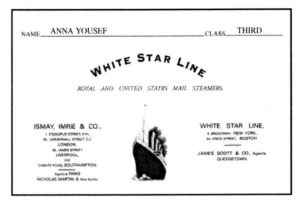

Grandma Anna: Often listed as Mrs. Darwin Touma (Thomas)

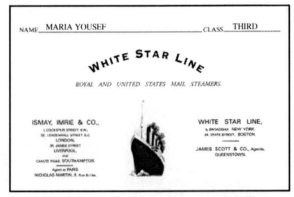

Maria Yousef: Often listed as Hanna Touma (Thomas)

NAME GEORGE YOUSEF   CLASS THIRD

WHITE STAR LINE

ROYAL AND UNITED STATES MAIL STEAMERS.

ISMAY, IMRIE & CO.,

WHITE STAR LINE,

JAMES SCOTT & CO., Agents, QUEENSTOWN.

George Yousef: Often listed as Master George Touma (Thomas)

ANNA THOMAS

After settling down in Dowagiac, Michigan, Anna gave birth to three more sons: Samual Thomas, Francis Thomas, and Joseph W. Thomas. Anna's husband, Darwin, passed away in 1945 at the age of 75. Anna outlived her daughter, Mary, and her son, Francis, (1965) before passing away in 1976 at the age of 91 years. Her oldest son, George, passed away in 1991, and her youngest son, Joseph, in 1995. In July of 1997, Samual Thomas joined his family on the last voyage to Dowagia, Michigan, U.S.A. He was 84 years old.

Back row:
George Thomas (Yousef) and Mary (Mary Yousef) Haddad
Front row standing: Samual Thomas, Joseph W. Thomas, and Francis Thomas
Front row seated:
Anna (Yousef) Thomas and husband, Darwin (Toma) Thomas
Seated in Darwin's lap: Emma Haddad, daughter of Mary (Maria)

29

Mary Haddad (Maria Yousef) and husband, Nicholas
circa. 1940s

MARY THOMAS HADDAD

Mary married Nicholas Haddad and gave birth to six children. Two daughters, Emma Haddad and Pearl Haddad. Four sons, William Haddad, Daniel Haddad, Jerry Haddad and Francis Haddad. Mary passed away in 1953 and her daughter Pearl passed away approximately 10 years later. Mary's husband Nicholas passed away a few years after Pearl. If Mary would still be alive today she would have many Titanic stories to tell to all of her grandchildren and great grandchildren. Her remaining children still reside in Michigan.

George Thomas (Yousef) and wife, Rose, 1926

GEORGE THOMAS

George married Rose in 1926 and was blessed with three children. Emily Thomas, Joseph L. Thomas, and Beatrice Thomas. In mid-1927, George left Dowagiac and went to Flint, Michigan, to work with his uncle Elias Rassey, Anna's brother, in the grocery business. He did well enough to purchase his

31

own business and sent for the entire family from Dowagiac.

His father and brothers helped in the store. He helped put his younger brother Joseph W. Thomas through medical college. After becoming a doctor, Joseph joined the army in World War II and also served in a MASH Unit in Korea before retiring after twenty years of service. George retired from the grocery business and went into the real estate investment business. In December of 1991 George passed away as the last survivor and left the legacy of the Titanic to the mercy of producers and directors. Rose passed away in 1997.

THE FINAL SUMMARY

In summary and in behalf of the Haddad and Thomas families, I would like to dedicate the proceeding story to our grandmother, Anna Thomas, for her courage, her foresight and the intuition she had shown throughout her ordeal traveling from far-off Tibnin to the United States. Had it not been for her, we would not exist today. She will remain in our hearts forever.

—JOSEPH L. THOMAS, GRANDSON

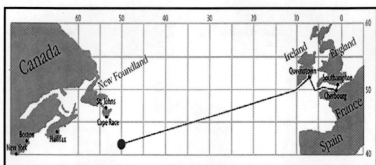

"The Titanic was expected to make a record on her maiden voyage. She made one unapproached in ocean annals; one which, it is hoped, may long stand unparalleled."

Incidents & Inquiries

BOAT NUMBER 2

British Report: Gives this as the seventh boat lowered from the Port Side at 1:45 A.M.

Inquiry and Affidavit's of survivors of Boat No.2 and questionings by U.S. Senators of Seasom Osman.

Passengers: Miss Allen (now Mrs. J. B. McMennell), Mrs. Appleton, Mrs. Cornell, Mrs. Douglas and maid (Miss Le Roy), Miss Madill, Mrs. Robert and maid (Amelia Kenchen). One third—class, foreigner, and family: Hanne Youssef and children Marian and Georges. The rest second and third-class.
Bade good-bye to wife and sank with ship: Mr. Douglas.
(Crew: Fourth Officer Boxhall, Seamen Osman and Steward Johnston, cook.
Total: 25.

J.G.Boxhall, Fourth Olilcer (Am. lnq., p. 240. and Br. lnq.):

I was sent away in Emergency boat 2, the last boat but one on the port side. There was one of the lifeboats (No. 4) lowered away a few minutes after I left. That was the next lifeboat to me aft. Englhardt boat "D" was being got ready. There was no anxiety of people to get into these boats. There were four men in this boat—a sailorman (Osman), a steward (Johnston), a cook and myself, and one male passenger who did not speak English—a middle-aged man with a black beard. He had his wife there and some children. When the order was given to lower the boat, which seemed to be pretty full, it was about twenty nuinutes to half an hour before the ship sank. Someone shouted through a megaphone: "Some of the boats come back and come around to the starboard side." All rowed except this male passenger. I handled one oar and a lady assisted me. She asked to do it. I got around to the starboard side intending to go alongside. I reckoned I could take about three more people off the ship with safety; and when about 22 yards off there was a little suction, as the boat seemed to be drawn closer, and I thought it would be dangerous to go nearer the ship. I suggested going back (after the ship sank) to the sailorrnan in the boat, but decided it was unwise to do so. There was a lady there, Mrs. Douglas, whom I asked to steer the boat according to my orders. She assisted me greatly in it. They told me on board the *Carpathia* afterwards that it was about ten minutes after four when we went alongside.

*William McMaster
Murdoch*

After we left the *Titanic* I showed green lights most of the time. When within two or three ship lengths of the *Carpathia,* it was just breaking daylight, and I saw her engines were stopped. She had stopped within half a mile or a quarter of a mile of an iceberg. There were several other bergs, and I could see field ice as far as I could see. The bergs looked white in the sun, though when we first saw them at daylight they looked black. This was the first time I had seen field ice on the Grand Banks. I estimate about 25 in my boat.

F. Osman, A. B. (Am. Inq., p. 538):

All of us went up and cleared away the boats. After that we loaded all the boats there were. I went away in No. 2, the fourth from the last to leave the ship. Boxhall was in command. Murdock directed the loading. All passengers were women and children, except one man, a third-class passenger, his wife and his two children. After I got in the boat the officer found a bunch of rockets which was put in the boat by mistake for a box of biscuits. The officer fired some off, and the *Carpathia* came to us first and picked us up half an hour before anybody else. Not until morning did we see an iceberg about 100 feet out of the water with one big point sticking out one side of it, apparently dark, like dirty ice, 100 yards away. I knew that was the one we struck. It looked as if there was a piece broken off.

There was no panic at all. There was no suction whatever. When we were in the boat I shoved off from the ship and I said to the officer: "See if you can get alongside to see if you can get some more hands— squeeze some more hands in"; so the women started to get nervous after I said that, and the officer said "All right." The women disagreed to that. We pulled around to the starboard side of the ship and found that we could not get to the starboard side because it was listing too far. We pulled astern again that way and after we lay astern we lay on our oars and saw the ship go down. It seemed to me as if all the engines and everything that was in the after part slid down into the forward part. We did not go back to the place where the ship had sunk because the women were all nervous, and we pulled around as far as we could get from it so that the women would not see and cause a panic. We got as close as we would dare to. We could not have taken any more hands into the boat. It was impossible. We might have gotten one in; that is all. There was no panic amongst the steerage passengers when we started mannning the boats. I saw several people come up from the steerage and go straight up to

36

the Boat Deck, and the men stood back while the women and children got into the boats—steerage passengers as well as others.

> *Senator Burton*: So in your judgement it was safer to have gone on the boat than to have stayed on the Titanic?
> *Witness*: Oh, yes, sir.
> *Senator Burton:* That was when you left?
> *Witness:* Yes, sir.
> *Senator Burton:* What did you think when the first boat was launched?
> *Witness:* I did not think she was going down then.

J. Johnson, steward (Br. Inq.):

Crew: Boxhall and four men, including perhaps Mr. McCullough. (None such on the list.) Boxhall said: " Shall we go back in the direction of cries of distress?" which were a half or three—quarters of a mile off. Ladies said: " No." Officer Boxhall signaled the *Carpathia* with lamp. Soon after launching, the swish of the water was heard against the icebergs. In the morning *Carpathia* on the edge of ice-field about 200 yards off.

Mrs. Walter D. Douglas's affidavit (Am. Inq., p. 1100):

Mr. Boxhall had difficulty in getting the boat loose and called for a knife. We finally were launched. Mrs. Appleton and a man from the steerage faced me. Mrs. Appleton's sister, Mrs. Cornell, was back of me and on the side of her, the officer. I think there were eighteen or twenty in the boat. There were many who did not speak English. The rowing was very difficult, for no one knew how. We tried to steer under Mr. Boxhall's orders, and he put an old lantern, with very little oil in it, on a pole, which I held up for some time. Mrs. Appleton and some other women had been rowing, and did row all the time. Mr. Boxhall had put into the Emergency boat a tin box of green lights like rockets. These he sent off at intervals, and very quickly we saw the lights of the *Carpathia,* whose captain said he saw our green lights ten miles away and steered directly towards us, so we were the first boat to arrive at the *Carpathia.* When we pulled alongside, Mr. Boxhall called out: *"Slow* down your engines and take us aboard. I have only one seaman."

Mrs. J. B. Mennell (née Allen):

My aunt, Mrs. Roberts' maid, came to the door and asked if she could speak to me. I went into the corridor and she said "Miss Allen. the baggage room is full of water." I replied she needn't worry, that the water-tight compartments would be shut and it would be all right for her to go back to her cabin. She went back and returned to us immediately to say her cabin, which was forward on Deck E, was flooded.

We were on the Boat Deck some minutes before being ordered into the lifeboat. Neither my aunt, Mrs. Roberts, my cousin, Miss Madill, nor myself ever saw or heard the band. As we stood there we saw a line of men file by and get into the boat—some sixteen or eighteen stokers. An officer came along and shouted to them: "Get out, you damned cowards; I'd like to see everyone of you overboard." They all got out and the officer said: "Women and children into this boat," and we got in and were lowered.

With the exception of two very harrowing leave-takings, we saw nothing but perfect order and quiet on board the *Titanic.* We were rowed round the stern to the starboard side and away from the ship, as our boat was a small one and Boxhall feared the suction. Mrs. Cornell helped to row all the time.

As the *Titanic* plunged deeper and deeper we could see her stern rising higher and higher until her lights began to go out. As the last lights on the stern went out we saw her plunge distinctively, bow first and intact. Then the screams began and seemed to last eternally. We rowed back, after the *Titanic* was under water, toward the place where she had gone down, but we saw no one in the water, nor were we near enough to any other lifeboats to see them. When Boxhall lit his first light the screams grew louder and then died down.

We could hear the lapping of the water on the icebergs, but saw none, even when Boxhall lit his green lights, which he did at regular intervals, till we sighted the *Carpathia*. Our boat was the first one picked up by the *Carpathia*. I happened to be the first one up the ladder, as the others seemed afraid to start up, and when the officer who received me asked where the *Titanic* was, I told him she had gone down.

Capt. A. H. Rostron, of the Carpathia:

We picked up the first boat, which was in charge of an officer who I saw was not under full control of his boat. He sang out that he had only one seaman in the boat, so I had to maneuver the ship to get as close to the boat as possible, as I knew well it would be difficult to do the pulling. By the time we had the first boat's people it was breaking day, and then I could see the remaining boats all around within an area of about four miles. I also saw icebergs all around me. There were about twenty icebergs that would be anywhere from about 150 to 200 feet high, and numerous smaller bergs; also numerous ones we call "growlers" anywhere from 10 to 12 feet high and 10 to 15 feet long, above the water.

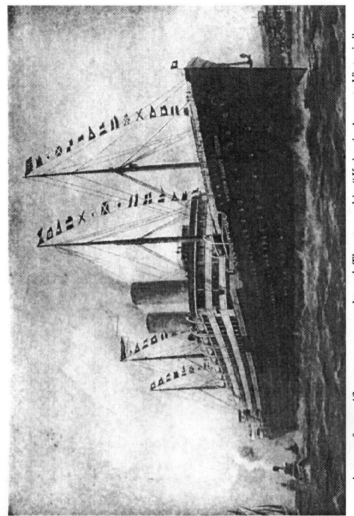

A type of magnificent ocean grey hound. The steamship "Kaiserin Auguste Victoria" of Hamburg-American Line.

United States Inquiry

INQUIRY BY UNITED STATES SENATE

L oading at the Rail—Inadequate Life-saving Appliances—No Extra Lookout—Searchlights Blinding—Wireless Rivals Not All Aroused—Went to Death in Sleep—Scratch Seamen—Cries of Agony—A Pitiful Story—Senators Ascertain Pertinent Facts—Much Good Accomplished.

What has been accomplished by the Senatorial inquiry into the loss of the Titanic with sixteen hundred lives?

For more than a week of the two that have elapsed since the Titanic made a record on her maiden voyage—a record never paralleled in marine history for its horrors, its sacrifice of life and material property—an earnest body of United States Senators has been at work conscientiously striving to uncover the facts, not alone for the purpose of placing the responsibility for what has now become one of the most heartrending chapters of all ocean history, but also in the hope of framing remedial legislation looking to the prevention of its recurrence.

The lead role in the US Senate investigation was played by Senator William Alden Smith, who performed most of the questioning

To attempt to draw conclusions as to the value of the work of a committee which is yet upon the threshold of its task would be presumptuous, but it is not too soon to present and formulate some of the pertinent facts, which its researches have established in the light of sworn evidence.

Any attempt at systematic analysis of the facts deduced from the many thousands of pages of testimony already taken naturally divided itself into two departments:

42

Were the Titanic's equipment and her general state of pre-
paredness such as to justify the broad claims made in her
behalf before the crisis arose, that she represented the acme
of human possibility not only in ocean going comfort and
speed but also in safety at sea?

Were the personnel and discipline of her officers and crew
of such a standard that, after the supreme crisis confronted
them, they utilized to the best advantage such facilities for
the safeguarding and preservation of life as remained at their
disposal?

With ten thousand families on both sides of the Atlantic
mourning the untimely death of relatives and friends who went
down into the depths from the decks of a brand new ship,
widely proclaimed the greatest and the safest that ever
ploughed the sea, these are, after all, the most pertinent questions that may be asked by a sorrowing world as it looks to
the future rather than the past.

LIFE-SAVING APPARATUS INADEQUATE

It has been demonstrated—and frankly conceded by the
company's managers and officers in the light of after knowledge—that the Titanic's life-saving appliances were woefully
inadequate to the safeguarding of even one-half her complement
of passengers and crew. On the day after the disaster was known
to the world it was shown that the ship's equipment of lifeboats
complied with the requirements of the English Board of Trade,
but that those requirements were so obsolete and antiquated that
they dated back to 1898 and were drafted to provide for vessels
of less than one-quarter the gross tonnage of the mammoth craft
of 46,000 tons of displacement.

The Titanic carried on her boat deck—sometimes referred
to as her sun deck—fourteen of the largest regulation size
lifeboats, seven on her port side and seven on the starboard.
Each of these had a carrying capacity, according to the Board
of Trade's established method of computation, of 65.5 per-

sons. Their aggregate capacity when afloat, therefore, was 917. The ship carried, in addition, four of the so-called collapsible boats and two others known as emergency boats—comparatively small craft employed in occasional duty—as when a man falls overboard.

The combined capacity of these six when afloat was hardly more than sufficient to care for two hundred persons. At the most liberal estimate, therefore, the entire equipment of boats aboard the great White Star liner might have afforded refuge, in the most favorable conditions, to less than 1,200 persons, or not quite half the number actually aboard the ship, on her maiden voyage.

In stating the lifeboat capacity the term "when afloat" has been used advisedly. One of the points which each of the Titanic's surviving officers has emphasized in evidence is the vast difference between loading with its human freight a boat that has been already placed in the water and loading one "at the rail," from a deck seventy feet above the water, with the subsequent perils of lowering it by means of the tackles sustaining its weight from bow and stern. Several of the officers

Nearly three dozen men clung to this overturned lifeboat for more than two hours.

have said that, in lowering loaded boats from the rail of the Titanic's boat deck, they would consider it unwise and even dangerous to fill the boats to more than one-half their rated capacity.

All the lifeboats that went away from the Titanic were loaded and lowered from the rail. Some of the smaller collapsible and emergency boats did not get away at all until the ship was so low in the water that they were simply pushed overboard, and one of them went over bottom up.

BOAT CARRIES 58 PERSONS

Harold G. Lowe, the fifth officer, commanded a boat which carried fifty-eight persons aboard. This, so far as is known, is the largest number of passengers carried in any of the lifeboats. Mr. Lowe testified that as his craft was lowered away from the davits he feared momentarily that, as a result of the tremendous strain upon her structure, she would buckle amidships and break before she reached the sustaining surface of the water, dropping all into the sea. "Had one more person leaped aboard her amidships as she was going down past the other decks," he said, "it might well have proved to be the last straw."

Mr. Lowe feared this might happen, as he saw steerage passengers "glaring at the boat" as it was lowered past the decks whereon they stood. It was for that reason, he explained to the investigating committee, that he discharged his revolver three times into the air as he and his boatload were dropping past the three lower decks. His purpose, he said, was to show that he was armed and to prevent any effort to overload the craft beyond a point which he already considered perilous.

Fifth Officer Harold G. Lowe

45

The canvas collapsible

C. H. Lightoller, second officer and ranking surviving officer of the Titanic, expressed the opinion that, in filling lifeboats from the Titanic's boat deck, "at the rail," it was involving serious risk to load them to more than half their rated capacity for filling while afloat. H, C. Boxhall, fourth officer, expressed a like view, but added that in an extreme emergency one man might take more chances than another.

In view of these expert opinions, it will be seen that, when it came to loading the Titanic's passengers into lifeboats "from the rail," the actual life-saving capacity of her available equipment was far less than the one thousand or eleven hundred that might have been carefully packed away into boats already resting safely on the surface of a calm sea.

A PUZZLING QUERY

And this consideration naturally suggests the query, *why were the Titanic's lifeboats all loaded "from the rail" of the topmost deck, at a point fully seventy feet above the sea?*

Why were they not lowered empty, or with only the necessary officers or crew aboard, and then filled with their quota of passengers, either from some lower deck, or else after they had reached the sustaining surface of the water?

It is evident that course was contemplated. Three of the surviving officers have testified that the available force of seamen was depleted after the ship struck, because a detail of men had been sent below to open up the gangway doors, for the purpose of embarking the passengers into the lifeboats from those outlets. There is nothing in evidence, as yet, to show that this purpose was ever accomplished, or to reveal the fate of the men sent to do the work.

Whether the men were unable or incompetent to force open the gangway doors, from which the lowered boats might easily have been filled, as the sea was as smooth as a mill pond; whether these outlets were jammed as a result of collision with the berg, or stuck because the ship's mechanisms were new, has not been revealed and may never be known.

Certain it is that all the lifeboats were loaded "from the rail," and their safe capacity was thereby reduced one-half in the judgment of the officers to whom their command was entrusted.

The inadequacy of the Titanic's lifeboat appliances is not disputed. Steamship companies are already vying with one another to correct in this respect the admitted shortcomings of the past. The sole excuse offered is that collision bulkheads, watertight compartments and other like devices have been regarded until now as making the marvelous vessels of the present day "their own best lifeboats." The Titanic and many of her sister ships of the ocean fleets have been called "unsinkable." They were generally believed to be so, and it is only since this greatest of disasters has shattered many illusions that marine engineers have confessed ruefully that the unsinkable ship has never yet been launched.

47

PERILS MINIMIZED

Since the day of the watertight compartment and of the wireless telegraph sea perils have been so minimized that in the most extreme of likely emergencies the function of the lifeboat had come to be regarded as that of an ocean ferry capable of transferring passengers safely and leisurely from an imperilled vessel to another standing by and co-operating in the task.

That was all the lifeboat had to do when the Republic sank. That was all they had to do years ago, when the Missouri, under Captain Hamilton Murrell's expert management, took off a thousand persons from a foundering ship without the loss of a single life. So it had come to be believed that the lifeboats would never be called upon to do more than that, and least of all in the case of the Titanic, latest and most superb of all the vessels built by man since the world began.

So deep rooted was this conviction in the minds of seagoing men that when Senator Smith, of Michigan, chairman of the investigating committee, asked one of the surviving officers: "What was the purpose of the Titanic carrying her fourteen full-size lifeboats?"

He naively replied: "To comply, I suppose, with the regulations of the London Board of Trade."

There has been no evidence to indicate that the Titanic lacked the proper number of life jackets, or life belts—one for every person aboard the ship—and it has not been proven that these life belts were not new and of proper quality and strength. Major Peuchen, of Toronto, one of the surviving passengers, however, in the course of his testimony, made two significant comments. He said that when the Carpathia, on the morning after the disaster, steamed through a lot of the Titanic's floating wreckage, he was surprised to note great quantities of broken bits of cork, such as are used in life preservers. He was astonished also that he did not see a larger number of floating bodies.

"I have always supposed," said Major Peuchen, who is an experienced yachtsman, "that a life preserver in good condition would sustain a dead body as well as a live one."

STEAMING AT 21 KNOTS

It has been demonstrated by ample evidence that at the time the Titanic hit the iceberg she was steaming at the undiminished speed of twenty-one knots an hour into a zone littered with icebergs and floating ice fields, warning of which her officers had received hours before by wireless from several other ships, including the Amerika, of the Hamburg-American Line. When day broke on Monday, according to Mr. Lane, at least twenty icebergs surrounded the Carpathia, the largest of which was 100 feet high. They were within a six-mile radius.

In the chart room, tucked into the corner of a frame above the table where the navigating officers of the Titanic did their mathematical work, was a written memorandum of the latitude and longitude wherein two large icebergs had been reported directly in the track. Mr. Boxhall had worked out this position under Captain Smith's instructions. Mr. Lightoller, the second officer, was familiar with it, and when his watch ended at 10 o'clock Sunday night and he surrendered the post on the bridge to the first officer, Mr. Murdoch, the remark was made that they would probably "be getting up into the ice during Mr. Murdoch's watch."

Despite all this, the Titanic was rushing on, driving at railroad speed toward the port of New York and "a record for a maiden voyage."

It was a cloudless and starlit night with no sea running. No extra lookout was posted in the "ship's eyes," the most advanced position on the vessel's deck. Up in the crow's nest Fleet and Lee, both experienced lookouts, were keeping a sharp watch forward. They had been duly warned of ice by

49

the pair of lookouts whom they had relieved.

UNAIDED BY SEA GLASSES

But the men in the crow's nest had to depend entirely upon the vision of the naked eye. They had no glass to aid them. Fleet had occupied a similar post of responsibility four years on the Oceanic without mishap. His testimony before the committee was that he never before had been without the aid of a glass. He had a pair of binoculars when the ship made her trial trip from Belfast, but they had been mislaid, and when the Titanic steamed out from Southampton he asked Mr. Lightoller for another pair and was told that there was no glass for him. Fleet's warning was too late to prevent the impact. His testimony was that with a glass he would have reported the berg in time to have prevented the ship striking it.

When Quartermaster Hitchens came on watch at 10 o'clock the weather had grown so cold that he, experienced seaman that he was, immediately thought of icebergs, though it was no part of his duty to look out for them. The thermometer showed thirty-one degrees, and the first orders he received were to notify the ship's carpenter to look to his fresh-water supply because of the freezing weather, and to turn on the steam-heating apparatus in the officers' quarters.

Still no extra lookout was placed and the men in the crow's nest were straining their tired eyes ahead without the help of a lens.

Captain Arthur Rostron, of the Carpathia, testified that when he was rushing his ship to the aid of the stricken Titanic, taking unusual chances because he knew lives were at stake, he placed a double watch on duty.

Each of the surviving officers, when he was questioned as to the Titanic's speed at a time when the proximity of dangerous ice was definitely reported and clearly indicated by the drop in temperature, said that it was "not customary" to slacken speed at such times, provided the weather was clear. The custom is, they said, "to go ahead and depend upon the lookouts in the crow's nest and the watch on the bridge to 'pick up' the ice in time to avoid hitting it."

Mr. Lowe, the fifth officer, who was crossing the Atlantic for the first time in his life, most of his fourteen years' experience at sea having been in the southern and eastern oceans, yawned wearily in the face of the examiner as he admitted that he had never heard that icebergs were common off the Banks of Newfoundland and that the fact would not have interested him if he had. He did not know that the Titanic was following what is known as "the southern track," and when he was asked, ventured the guess that she was on the northerly one.

MIGHT HAVE BEEN SAVED BY SEARCHLIGHT

Questions framed by Senator Smith several times have suggested that the use of a searchlight might have saved the Titanic. War ships of all nations make the searchlight a part of their regular equipment, as is well known. The Titanic's surviving officers agreed that it has not been commonly used by vessels of the merchant marine. Some of them conceded that in the conditions surrounding the Titanic its use on a clear night might have revealed the iceberg in time to have saved the ship. Major Peuchen, of Toronto, said emphatically that it would have done so.

Mr. Lightoller, however, pointed out that, while the searchlight is often a useful device for those who stand behind it, its rays invariably blind those upon whom they are trained. Should the use of searchlights become general upon merchant vessels, he thought, it would be a matter for careful consideration, experiment and regulation.

The Senatorial inquiry has indicated that the single lifeboat drill upon the Titanic had been a rather perfunctory performance; there had been neither a boat drill nor a fire drill from the time the great ship left Southampton until she struck the iceberg. While she lay in harbor before starting on her maiden voyage, and with her port side against the company pier, two of her lifeboats had been lowered away from her starboard side, manned by a junior or a warrant officer and a crew of four men each, who rowed them around a few minutes and then returned to the ship.

There had also been an inspection in the home port to see whether the lifeboats contained all the gear specified by the Board of Trade regulations and Officer Boxhall testified that they did. Yet, when the emergency came, many of the boats were found to contain no lights, while others lacked extra oars, biscuits and other specified requisites.

UTILITY OF WATER-TIGHT COMPARTMENTS DOUBTED

According to company claims, these doors could be closed instantly from the bridge, or automatically if the deck below flooded.

The Titanic's loss has completely exploded the fallacy that watertight compartments, of which the big ship had fifteen in her main divisions, can save a vessel from foundering after having sustained a raking blow, tearing and ripping out her plates from thirty feet aft of the bow almost to midships.

Mr. Lightoller expressed the belief under oath that the star-

52

board side of the Titanic had been pierced through compartments 1, 2, 3 and probably 4, numbering from the collision bulkhead toward the midship section. The testimony of Quartermaster Hitchins showed that the vessel filled so fast that when the captain looked at the commutator five minutes after the ship struck, the Titanic showed a list of five degrees to starboard. Rushing water drove the clerks out of the mail room before they could save their letter bags.

One reform that is likely to take shape early as a result of the Senatorial investigation is a more thorough regulation of wireless telegraphy both in shore stations and on ships at sea. Interference by irresponsible operators will probably be checked by governmental action, and the whole subject may come up for uniform international regulation in the Berlin conference.

It is conceded that on all ships the receiving apparatus of the wireless instruments should be manned at all hours of the day and night, just as are the ship's bridge and the engine rooms. The Senate inquiry has showed that had the death call of the Titanic gone out five minutes later it would never have reached the Carpathia, whose one wireless operator was about to retire for the night when he heard the signal that took the Cunarder to the rescue of the seven hundred who survived.

There has been shown, too, grave need of some cure for the jealousies and rivalries between competing systems of wireless. To the Frankfurt, which was one of the nearest, if not the nearest, of the several ships to the sinking Titanic, her operator sent the curt message, "Shut up !" From the Californian the operator refused to take a message, which proved to be an ice warning, because "he was busy with his accounts." With the sanction of high officers of their company wireless operators have suppressed vital public information for the purpose of commercializing their exclusive knowledge for personal profit.

So much for the Titanic's boasted equipment—or the lack

of it. There remains to be summarized the evidence adduced as to the personnel and discipline, as these were indicated by what occurred after the ship confronted the direst of all emergencies.

The Titanic was expected to make a record on her maiden voyage. She made one unapproached in ocean annals; one which, it is hoped, may long stand unparalleled.

British Inquiry, 1912

THE BRITISH INQUIRY OF 1912

The sittings of the Court of Inquiry appointed by the Gov ernment to investigate and report upon the loss of the "Titanic" are now being held, with Lord Mersey as President. They opened on May 2nd and the Attorney-General (Sir Rufus Isaacs, K.C., M.P.), who is leading counsel for the Board of Trade, read to the Court at its first sitting a list of the questions which it was proposed to submit. One of the questions to be submitted was:

What installations for receiving and transmitting messages by wireless telegraphy were on board the "Titanic"? How many operators were employed in working such installations? Were the installations in good and effective working order, and were the number of operators sufficient to enable messages to be received and transmitted continuously by day and night?

There is no need to deal here with the general evidence and the intricate mass of detail which is being unravelled at al-

The British inquiry was, headed by Lord Mersey, the Wreck Commissioner.

most every step. It will suffice to confine ourselves to the evidence bearing upon the working of the wireless, which has been compiled for this journal from, reports in *The Times* and other newspapers, The Marconi Company are in no way resonsible for any of the statements made.

Here, as we have been reminded again and again, for hours together were ships ploughing the oceans hundreds and thousands of miles from land, and, for that matter, hundreds of miles from each other, advising one another, as it in the most customary, everyday way, of the presence of ice in the North Atlantic—passing the word, so to speak, from mouth to mouth.

Mr. Cyril Evans, examined by the Solicitor-General on May 15th, stated that he was the sole Marconi operator in the "Californian." At 5.35 p.m. New York time, or 7.30 ship's time, he received a message from the steamship "Antillian" that an hour before she had seen three large icebergs to south-ward. A little later he heard from the "Titanic" and offered her the report about the ice, and she replied, "All right, I heard the same thing from the 'Antillian.'" At 9.5 New York time, or 11 o'clock ship's time, the captain directed him to tell the "Titanic" that the "Californian" was stopped and surrounded by ice. He sent the message to the "Titanic" and got the reply, " Keep out." That was because the "Titanic" was at that mo-ment in communication with Cape Race, and his message had caused an interruption. The "Titanic," however, must have heard what he had said about the ice, because his signals were much stronger and louder than the Cape Race signals. He next heard the "Titanic" say to Cape Race, "Sorry, please re-peat." The messages from the "Titanic" to Cape Race were private messages from the passengers.

The witness was then examined in regard to the visit paid to his room by Mr. Stewart, the chief officer, at ten minutes to 6 o'clock ship's time. Mr. Stewart said to him, "There's a ship been firing rockets: will you please try to find out whether there is anything the matter"?

The witness immediately jumped out of his bunk and took up the telephones, but he could hear nothing. He then sent out a general call, and got an answer from the "Mount Temple" saying, "Do you know the 'Titanic' struck an iceberg and is sunk?" The "Frankfurt" also sent him the same message. At this time Mr. Stewart was in the room. When he heard the messages frm the "Mount Temple" and the "Frankfurt" he wrote down the position on a piece of paper and gave it to the captain. Then he asked the Allan liner "Virginian," which was coming from Cape Race, for an official message, and she gave it as follows: "Titanic" struck berg, wants assistance, urgent, passengers in boats, ship sinking. Position 41.46 N., 50.14 W. Gamble, Commander.

In cross-examination the witness said he judged by the strength of the "Titanic's" signals that she was not more than 100 miles away from the "Californian" in the afternoon. They had instructions to communicate with all ships in cases of distress.

Captain Henry Moore, master of the Canadian Pacific Railway steamer "Mount Temple," 6,661 tons, was the next witness. He described the receiving of the "Titanic's" "C.Q.D." message on the morning of April 15th, and how he immediately put the ship round and steered east.

Mr. John Durrant, Marconi operator of the "Mount Temple," was the next witness. In reply to the Solicitor-General, he stated that the range of his wireless installation was 150 miles by day and 200 miles by night. On the evening of Saturday, April 13th—the day before the foundering of the "Titanic" he got an official message from the captain of the "Corinthian" to the captain of the "Mount Temple" that ice had been seen. This was the only message he received in regard to ice before the wreck.

The witness then proceeded to give from his log-book the various calls he heard sent out by the "Titanic" and the replies to them by ships which they reached.

The first thing he heard of the "Titanic" was at 11 past 12 o'clock (ship's time) on Sunday night, when he got the message "C.Q.D." from the "Titanic," giving her position, and adding, "Come at once. Struck berg. Advise captain." He told his captain at once. After the lapse of ten minutes he had the entry, " 'Titanic' still calling C.Q.D.,". that she was asked by the "Carpathia" what was wrong, and replied, Struck iceberg. Come to our position," which was given. At 12.26 a.m. he made the entry— "'Titanic' still calling C.Q.D." At this time the "Mount Temple" had altered her course, and was speeding to the assistance of the "Titanic." This had been done about 15 minutes after getting the first signal. At 12.34 he heard the "Frankfurt" answering the "Titanic," and the "Titanic" giving her position to the "Frankfurt." The "Titanic" asked, "Are you coming to our assistance?" The "Frankfurt" said, "What is the matter with you?" and the " Titanic" answered, "Have struck an ice berg. Sinking. Come to our help. Tell captain." The "Frankfurt" then said, "O.K. Will tell bridge at once," and the "Titanic" replied, "O.K. Yes. Ouick." At 12.42 he heard the "Titanic" calling "S.O.S."

At a quarter to 1 o'clock he heard the "Titanic" sending out both calls. She then got into touch with the "Carpathia," and next with the "Virginian."

The Solicitor-General: If you had broken in and talked to the "Titanic" you would have interrupted her messages to other ships?

— Yes, I never said a word after I got her position. The first rule in wireless telegraphy is " Never interfere."

The witness, continuing the narrative from his log-book, said the "Titanic" called the "Olympic" at 12.43 a.m. The "Olympic" replied at 1.06 a.m., and got the message, "Get your boats ready. Going down fast by the head." At 1.13 the "Frankfurt" sent a message to the "Titanic," "Our captain will go for you." At 1.13 he heard the "Titanic" working the "Baltic."

The witness said the "Titanic" answered the "Olympic," We are putting the women all in the boats," At 1.29 the "Titanic" sent out a general call, "C.Q.D. Engine-room flooded." The "Titanic" also informed the "Olympic" that the sea was clear and calm. At 1.31 he heard the "Frankfurt" say to the "Titanic," are there any boats round you already? and to this the "Titanic" made no reply. At 1.33 he heard the "Olympic" send a message to the "Titanic," asking whether the "Titanic" was steering south to meet the "Olympic," and the reply of

59

the "Titanic" was simply the code word for "Received." That was the last message that he heard from the "Titanic." The messages from the "Titanic" did not get fainter towards the end. When the messages ceased, he thought the flooding of the engine-room had put the wireless out of condition. Most ships, including his own, carried storage batteries for use when power could not be obtained from the dynamos, and the wireless apparatus could be changed from the dynamos to the storage batteries in a minute; but time range of a wireless using storage batteries would be less than that of a wireless using dynamos.

At 1.41 a.m. he heard the "Frankfurt" and the Russian ship, the "Birma," calling the "Titanic," and there was no re-

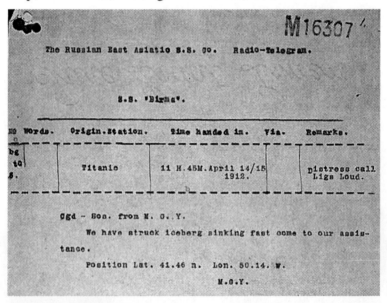

M16307

The Russian East Asiatic S.S. Co.   Radio-Telegram.

S.S. 'Birma'.

No Words.	Origin.Station.	Time handed in.	Via.	Remarks.
	Titanic	11 H.45M.April 14/15 1912.		Distress call Ligs Loud.

Cgd - Bos. from M. G. Y.

We have struck iceberg sinking fast come to our assistance.

Position Lat. 41.46 n.   Lon. 50.14. W.

M.G.Y.

ply. At 1.56 the "Olympic," the "Frankfurt," and the "Baltic" called, and again there was no answer from the "Titanic." At 2.11 the "Birma" informed the "Frankfurt" that she was 70 miles from the "Titanic." At 2.36 he made the entry, All quiet now. The "Titanic" has not. spoken since 1.33." At 3.11 he heard the "Carpathia" say, "If you are there, we are firing rockets." At 3.26 the "Carpathia" again called the "Titanic." At 3.44 the "Birma" told the "Frankfurt" that he thought he heard the "'Titanic," and calling her, said, "Steaming full speed to you. Shall arrive 6 in the morning. Hope you are safe. We are only 50 miles away." At 3.46 he heard the "Carpathia" calling again. At 4.46 he made the entry, "All quiet. We are stopped away. Pack ice." At 5.11 the "Californian" called, "C.Q.," and he answered, telling her that the "Titanic" had struck an iceberg and sunk, and he gave her the position. At 5.26 he heard the "Californian"speaking to the "Frankfurt," and the "Frankfurt" replied to the same effect. His last entry was, 8 am. Heard from "Carpathia" that she had rescued 20 boatloads."

Witness denied that he heard any message to the effect that the "Titanic" was steaming to Halifax, or that all passengers had been rescued.

Captain James Barr, of the "Caronia," was on May 17th examined in relation to a warning as to ice which he sent to the "Titanic" at 9 o'clock on the morning of Sunday, April

Had it not been for the wireless operators in the "Marconi Room," most of Titanic's passengers would probably have been lost to the frigid water.

14th. The marconigram he sent was in the following terms: "West-bound steamers report bergs, growlers, and field ice in 42 N. and 49 to 51W." At 9.45 he received the following reply: "Thanks for message and information. Have had variable weather throughout.—SMITH."

On May 22nd Mr. G. E. Turnhull, the deputy-manager of the Marconi International Marine Communication Company, was called to prove from the records of "La Touraine," the "Caronia," the "Amerika," the "Baltic," the "Californian" and the "Mesaba" the warning messages which were said to have been sent to the "Titanic."

He explained that the records of wireless messages sent or received by a ship with the Marconi installation were sent to the offices of the company at the end of the voyage. The *proces verbal,* or diary of messages, kept in the Marconi office in the "Caronia" showed that on April 14th Captain Barr sent a warning message as to ice to the "Titanic " at 1.26 p.m. It was acknowledged in the following terms: "Thanks for information. We have had variable weather throughout.— Smith."

The wireless message from the German steamer "Amerika" on April 14th reporting that she had passed two large icebergs was intended for the Hydrographic Office at Washington. It happened that at the moment the "Amerika" sent out the message she was not within the range of communication with Cape Race, but she was within the range of communication with the "Titanic," which, in turn, was within the range of communication with Cape Race and, therefore, the "Amerika" asked the "Titanic" to forward the message to Cape Race. Mr. Turnboll said that he had sent two telegrams to the wireless station at Cape Race asking them to state whether they had received on April 14th a message from the "Amerika" via the " Titanic," and to say whether they got the message direct from the "Titanic" or through another ship. The answer he received was as follows: "Received direct from

"Titanic," April 14th, steamship 'Amerika,' via 'Titanic.' 'Amerika' passed two large icebergs in 41.27 N., 50.8 W., on April 14th."

The President: That, at present, satisfies me that this message had reached the Marconi operator in the "Titanic," was read by him, and transmitted by him to Amerika, but there it stops.

Witness added that the receipt of the message from the "Amerika" by the "Titanic" involved its being written down by the operator on board the "Titanic."

The Solicitor-General: Will you tell me what is the practice of your operators in the case of a message of this sort passing through the "Titanic?" Do they treat it as a message which concerns the ship from which it is transmitted?

—In ordinary practice it would be treated as a private message, but the operator, seeing from the contents of it how important it was as regards the navigation of the ship, would, without any doubt whatever, communicate its contents to the commander or officers.

The President: You mean by that that you think he ought to do so?

—It is the general practice.

Have you ever been in one of these steamers in the Marconi room?

—I have. I made a trip to America in 1904.

Can you recall any case where you received a private message which you thought would be of interest to the captain of the ship you were upon, and which you disclosed to the captain of that ship?

—No; I cannot recall any particular instance.

Mr. Turnbull then produced the, *proces verbal* of the "Baltic," which showed that the following message was sent at 11.52 a.m. on April 14th to Captain Smith of the "Titanic."

Have had moderate, variable winds and clear, fine weather since leaving. Greek steamer reports passing icebergs and large

quantity field ice in latitude 41.51 N., longitude 49.52 W. Last night we spoke German steamer 'Deutschland,' Stettin to Philadelphia, not under control, short of coal, latitude 40.42 N., longitude 55.11 W. Wishes to be reported at New York and other steamers. Wish you and "Titanic" all success.
—COMMANDER."

The reply of the captain of the " Titanic" to this message was, the witness said, received at 12.55 p.m., and was in these terms: "Thanks for your message and good wishes. Had fine weather since leaving.—SMITH."

The witness added that the time given in both messages was New York time, and ship's time would be about two hours later.

Sir Robert Finley: (who appeared for the White Star Line): This is the first we have heard of this message.

The President: Do you dispute receiving it?

Sir Robert Finley: I do not know anything about it. I have not heard of it until this moment.

The Solicitor-General then put in an affidavit made by the captain of the "Baltic" in relation to another message sent to the "Titanic." This was to the effect that on April 14th reports were received by wireless telegraphy from numbers of steamships of having passed ice and bergs in positions varying from 49.9 W., to 50.20 W. on the outward southern track. These ice reports were, in the ordinary course, sent out by the operator to all other ships with wireless apparatus, including the "Titanic." They were sent shortly before noon, New York time. The operator received an acknowledgment from the "Titanic" about 1 p.m., New York time, on the same day.

Mr. Turnbull said that in the *proces verbal* of the "Baltic" there was no record of any message but the message he had mentioned having been sent by the "Baltic" to the "Titanic."

The Solicitor-General pointed out that the report of the evidence given at the American inquiry showed that the captain of the" Baltic" stated that he received more ice messages than one.

The President said he did not doubt that. But that these messages were sent out to the "Titanic," in the sense of having been received by the "Titanic," did not seem to be accurate.

The Solicitor-General said, as regarded the "Californian," they had already evidence from the operator Evans, of that ship regarding the warning of three large bergs—a warning despatched at 7.30 p.m. on Sunday, ship's time. Evans was sending to the "Antillian," and was told by the "Titanic" operator that he had overheard it.

The President: There is nothing in writing, as far as I know, to show that this "Californian" message was received by Captain Smith?

Sir Robert Finley: No.

The Solicitor-General next mentioned the warning sent by the "Mesaba" (Atlantic Transport Line), which, he said, was the "critical message."

Sir Robert Finley: This we say we did not receive.

The President: Yes; but the "Californian" overheard it.

The witness produced the record of the "Mesaba's" message. There was first a "Time Rush" message, dated 7.50 New York time, stating that an ice report had been sent to the "Titanic." Mr. Turnbull explained that a "Time Rush" message was a preliminary telegram to inform a ship of the telegrams ready to be despatched for it. He then read the message, dated 7.50 p.m., and sent by S. H. Adams, the "Mesaba's" operator, to the "Titanic" Ice report—In latitude 42 N. to 41.25 N., longitude 49 W. to 50.30 W., saw much heavy pack ice and great number of large icebergs, also field ice. Weather good, clear." At the bottom of the same form there appeared this entry by the "Mesaba's" operator: "Reply received, thanks. Sent this to about ten other ships as well; names in P.V. *(proces verbal)."* The reply, Mr. Turnbull explained, would be sent by the "Titanic's" operator, not by the captain.

Mr. H. Bride was then called and examined by the Attorney-General. He said that in June, 1911, he obtained his certificate of proficiency in radial telegraphy from the Postmaster-General, and later on he was appointed by the Marconi Company to serve as assistant wireless operator in the "Titanic." He joined the "Titanic" at Belfast in the beginning of April. On the trial trip of the ship from Belfast to Southampton, Phillips, the senior operator, and he tested the wireless apparatus with several stations on the mainland and found it in good working order. The arrangement as to the watches they had made was that Phillips was to go on duty from 8 o'clock at night till two in the morning, and the witness from 2 o'clock in the morning until eight. During the, day they took turns to suit one another's convenience. But a continuous and constant watch was kept, and one or other of them was always in the Marconi room, which was close to the bridge.

Will you tell us as far as you are able what was the first message you recollect with regard to ice?

—The first message I recollect on April 14th was from the "Californian."

That was the first you recollect?

—And the last. Had you any messages before the 14th?

—No, sir.

What was the message you recollect receiving on the 14th? Do you recollect the time?

—The time was between 5 and 5.30 in the afternoon, ship's time. It stated that the "Californian" was passing close to a large iceberg. She gave the latitude and longitude.

Was that a message intended for you or which you overheard?

—It was a message which was intended for me in the first place and which I overheard afterwards.

Do you always write the messages down which you receive?

—Yes, sir.

Is that an invariable practice?

—Invariable.

Do you also write the messages which you send?

—They are generally written for us.

And put before you for transmission?

—Yes, sir.

The witness added that to the best of his recollection the message from the "Californian" which he overheard was intended for the "Baltic," and was acknowledged by the "Baltic." At the time he overheard this message he was aware that the "Californian" had the same message for the "Titanic."

The Attorney-General read an extract from the evidence given by Bride in America to the effect that the message from the "Californian" which he had overheard was that they had seen three large bergs five miles to the southward of them; and that it was sent to the "Antillian."

The witness said he might have had it in his mind when he reached New York that the message was sent to the "Antillian." He was very busy on the Sunday, and had had many communications.

The Attorney General: What did you do when you got this message from the "Californian"?

—I delivered it to the officer on the bridge.

Do you remember who the officer on the bridge was?

—No; I was not acquainted with the officers.

Can you tell us how long it was after you got the message that you delivered it to the bridge?

—Two minutes.

Did it strike you as an important message?

—That sort of message is looked upon as important.

The President asked whether there was any doubt that this message did come to the knowledge of the officers on the bridge.

Sir Robert Finley: I think there is no doubt at all. The point is—when?

67

The Attorney General: This witness says two minutes after it was received.

(To the witness): From the time you received that message until the "Titanic" sank, as far as you are concerned, there was no other ice eported?

—No, sir.

Did you have any conversation at all with Mr. Phillips about ice messages?

—No, sir.

The witness said he was relieved by Phillips between 6 and 7 o'clock—to the best of his recollection—in order that he might go down to dinner.

The witness said, in reply to the Attorney-General, that when he did come up from dinner he had a conversation with

This iceberg was photographed approximately 100 miles north of where the Titanic disaster took place.

Phillips in the Marconi room. Phillips established communication with Cape Race between 8.30 and 9 o'clock.

The President asked how did he know that Phillips established communication with Cape Race at that time?

The witness said that he had "turned in," and as his sleeping place adjoined the instrument room he could read by sound the messages that Phillips was sending to Cape Race.

The President remarked that the witness's memory appeared to be so extraordinarily accurate as to time that, while he did not say the witness was not telling the truth, he wondered whether he could really remember details so distinctly.

The witness said he remembered these things because they constituted his work.

Replying to the Attorney-General, he said he particularly remembered communication being established with Cape Race. It was very important that they should get into communication with Cape Race because there was a large accumulation of messages awaiting despatch.

The President said that would explain how the witness remembered so well.

The witness proceeded to say that he relieved Phillips at 12 o'clock midnight—two hours before he was regularly due—because Phillips had had a busy time the night before. That was after the collision. Phillips then told him that he had cleared off the traffic to Cape Race, but Phillips did not say when he had actually completed the work. It was not until then that the witness heard that there had been a collision. He was asleep at the time of the impact.

Phillips told him he thought the ship had struck something from the feel of the shock that followed. They were not then sending or receiving messages. The captain came into the Marconi room shortly afterwards and said he wanted assistance from other vessels. Mr. Phillips was told to be quick about it, so he set about sending "C.Q.D." imniediately. Answers were received from the "Frankfurt" and the "Carpathia."

The "Frankfurt" wired, "O.K. (all right), stand by" (*i.e.*, wait for further reply). The "Frankfurt" gave no position. The "Carpathia" transmitted her position, said she had turned, and was coming along as fast as possible. The "Olympic" sent several messages right up to the time when they finally left the cabin, but he believed they were! not delivered, because they presumed that Captain Smith was busy. The effect of one of the messages was to tell Captain Smith to have his lifeboats ready. He went to report to the captain, who was on the boat deck superintending the lowering of the lifeboats. Later, the captain came into the Marconi room and told them the ship would not last very long, and that the engine-room was flooded. Mr. Phillips thought that the "Frankfurt" was the nearer of the two vessels, as the strength of the "Frankfurt's" signals was greater than that of the "Carpathia's." He informed the "Baltic" that they had had a collision and were sinking fast. Mr. Phillips had then gone outside to look round, and when he came back he said that the fore well-deck was awash, and that they were putting the women and the children in the boats and clearing off. Then the captain came in and told them to shift for themselves, because the ship was sinking.

Were you at that time called up?

—Yes, Mr. Phillips took the telephones up when the captain had gone away and started to work again. He could read what Phillips was sending, but not what he was receiving, and he judged that the "Carpathia" and the "Frankfurt" had both called up together; the "Frankfurt" had persisted in calling them, and was interfering with Mr. Phillips's reading of the "Carpathia's" message. Mr. Phillips expressed his opinion of the "Frankfurt," and told the operator of that vessel "to keep out of it and stand by." Mr. Phillips then told the "Carpathia" that they were abandoning the ship, Mr. Phillips tried to call once or twice more, but the power (which they got from the engine-room) was failing, and they failed to get any replies.

Then he and Phillips lined up on top of the Marconi cabin in the officers' quarters. They were trying to fix up a collapsible boat, and he helped to get it down from the top deck to "A" deck. He got into it, but as the vessel sank it was floated off upside down. He was swept off the boat deck. When he last saw Mr. Phillips he was standing on the deck-house. The witness said he swam away from the collapsible boat, but he joined it three-quarters of an hour later.

Mr. Lightoller, one of the ship's officers, was then recalled, and said, in answer to Sir H. Finlay, that he never heard anything whatever of the message which was said to have been sent from the "Mesaha," and which should have reached them before 10 p.m. He also had heard nothing of the message supposed to have been sent from the "Amerika."

What is the custom with regard to messages which are communicated by the Marconi operators to the captain?

—It is customary for the messages to be sent direct to the bridge. If addressed to Captain Smith they are delivered to him personally when he is in the quarters or on the bridge. If Captain Smith is not immediately available, either in his room or on the bridge, they were then delivered to the senior officer of the watch. Captain Smith's instructions were to open all telegrams and act on your own discretion.

And are you positive that you never heard anything?

—Absolutely positive.

The witness said that he saw the captain on the bridge on the night of the disaster from 8.55 to 9.20.

A message such as that from the "Mesaba" would be one that would be communicated to him?

—I have no doubt that it would be immediately communicated to him if it referred to pack ice.

In answer to the Solicitor-General, Mr. Lightoller said he had a distinct recollection of captain Smith's bringing a message to him on the bridge at about 12.45 p.m. on Sunday.

There were perhaps other messages, but he could not recollect with any distinctness having seen them.

Mr. Lightoller was examined with reference to the calculation he made on the day of the casualty that they would be up to the ice region by 9.30 p.m. whereas Mr. Moody had calculated that they would not reach it until 11 p.m. He said he had come to the conclusion that Mr. Moody in forming that estimate did not take the same wireless telegram that Captain Smith had shown to him (Mr. Lightoller).

The Solicitor-General: If you take the "Baltic's" marconigram you would, according to that, be up to the ice about 11 o'clock. Did you know that?

—No, I did not.

You know the "Caronia" mentioned that you would get to the ice on the 49th meridian. And your impression at the time was, not that Mr. Moody had made a mistake in his calculation, but that he had used another marconigram?

—Exactly.

The "Baltic's" message would reach the "Titanic" about 1 p.m. Do you observe that if you told Mr. Moody at 6 p.m. about the ice message, the "Baltic" message would be a later message in point of time than the "Caronia's"?

—I see. But my instructions to Mr. Moody would direct him to look for the easternmost ice.

Mr. Lightoller added that he heard nothing of the

COLLISION WITH ICEBERG – Apr 14 – Lat 41° 46', lon 50° 14', the British steamer TITANIC collided with an iceberg seriously damaging her bow; extent not definitely known.

Apr 14 – The German steamer AMERIKA reported by radio telegraph passing two large icebergs in lat 41° 27', lon 50° 08'.--TITANIC (Br ss).

Apr 14 – Lat 42° 06', lon 49° 43', encountered extensive field ice and saw seven icebergs of considerable size.--PISA (Ger ss).

J. J. KNAPP

Captain, U. S. Navy
Hydrographer.

"Californian's" message at all.

The President: The "Caronia's" telegram would indicate that the ice was to the north of the track?

—I believe so.

Is it possible that Mr. Moody may have calculated the position of the ice as given by the "Baltic"?

—It is possible, but it is most probable that he would pay greatest attention to the longitude, regardless of the latitude.

But if he did, calculating from the "Baltic's" telegram, he would ascertain the time at which the ice would be reached as 11 o'clock?

— Quite so.

And the "Baltic's" information was to the effect that the ice was just on the track?

— Yes, a little to the north.

The Solicitor-General asked the witness where, supposing there was a message about ice which could not be given personally to the captain, such a message would be placed.

The witness said it would be brought to the senior officer of the watch on the bridge. He added that his explanation of the chit of paper on the chart-room table, with the word "ice" on it, was that an officer had noted from some telegram an ice position and had scribbled it on paper, and had merely left the paper lying there, instead of crumpling it up, after pricking off the position on the chart.

The President: Can you tell me what other ice messages besides the "Caronia's" you heard of?

The witness: None that I remember.

Mr. Boxhall, Mr. Pitnian and Mr. Lowe were recalled and questioned upon the number of messages received relating to ice.

Mr. Boxhall said he remembered writing out the chart, which gave the position of the ice reported by the "Caronia." He never heard anything of a message from the "Mesaba" until the night they reached New York. He then heard that some one who had been talking to the captain of the "Mesaha" was told that the ship had warned them. So far as he knew there was no message received by any officer on the bridge during his watch from 8 o'clock to 12 o'clock. Captain Smith was frequently on the bridge during the watch.

The Solicitor-General: Did you know of more than one ice message?

The witness: I recall messages from the "Caronia" and "La Touraine," and there was another shortly after.

The inquiry stands adjourned.

Pictorial Section

Reproduced from the book
"The Story of The Titanic; As Told By Its Survivors"
Lawrence Beesley, Archibald Gracie,
Commander Lightoller, Harold Bride

Edited by Jack Winocour

Dover Publications, Inc. New York

Triple screw steamer "Titanic" was the largest vessel in the world"
882.5 feet long, 45,000 tons register, and 92.5 feet wide

The Titanic narrowly escapes collision with the steamer New York in Southampton.

*The Titanic carried four funnels such as the one above, one of which
fell upon scores of people struggling
in the water as the ship sank.*

Captain Edward John Smith did all he could to save women and children and then, in the true spirit of the sea, went down with his ship.

*(from left to right) Charles A. Bartlett, Henry Tringle Wilde
and Captain Edward John Smith*

80

Entrance hall and main staircase on the Titanic. The entrance hall and main staircase was located in the forward section and displayed the beauty and magnificence of the great ship. It was the largest steamship in the world.

This is part of the grand concert room, where women gathered and spent much of their time reading and listening to music

This is a luxuriously furnished smoking room where men spent many special social hours before the tragic event in early April, 1912

Another rendering of the first-class smoking room which reflects the dignity of a private club.

The grand dining saloon and restaurant shown above is a far-cry more luxurious than the facilities offered to the third-class steerage passengers depicted below

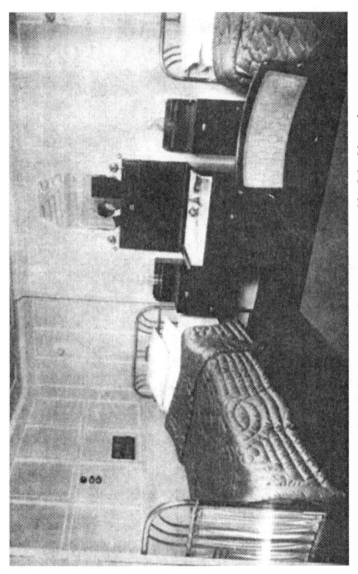

One of the Deluxe rooms such as were occupied by John Mr. and Mrs.Jacob Astor and many other millionaires aboard Titanic

Scene on the upper deck of the Titanic showing the lifeboats and newly invented davits(insert). These davits were designed to handle three times the number of boats the Titanic carried. Had there been enough of the lifeboats most, if not all of the passengers would have survived the Titanic's disaster at sea.

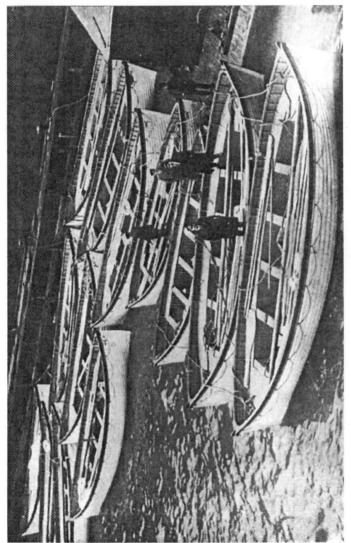

These lifeboats from the Titanic could only accommodate about a third of the passengers. These few boats rescued all that were saved from the disaster.

View of the promenade deck on Titanic. The deck extends nearly the entire length of the ship and was used as a promendae for the passengers

*Col. John Jacob Astor, Grandson of
the founder of the Astor family in
America, after putting his bride in
one of the lifeboats he remained
aboard the ill-fated ship and
died as a hero.*

89

J. Bruce Ismay, White Star Line Manager, who was severely criticised for his actions in connection with the sinking of the Titanic. It was he who ordered Captain Smith to proceed at maximum speed, knowing there icebergs in the area.

Major Archibald Butt was a military aid to presidents Roosevelt and Taft. He was a starch advocate for "women and children first" and after seeing the last lifeboat safely away he, too, went down with the Titanic.

91

Isadore Strause, millionaire and philanthropist, along with his wife, Ilda, who would not leave her husband's side, became legend in the Titanic's last minutes.

William T. Stead of London, England, was the editor of "Review of Reviews," nobly stood with Captain Smith as the great ship went down.

*Colonel Archibald Gracie was a member of the wealthy Gracie family
of New York state. One of Gracie's ancestors built Gracie Mansion
which became the official residence of the Mayor of
New York City in 1942.*

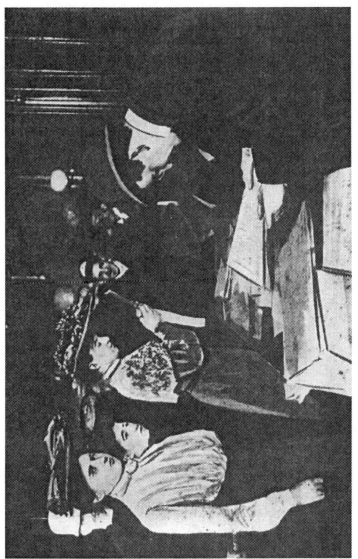

Survivors and family members searching for lost friends and relatives at the steamship company.

Effect of a mirage that can be seen within the ice floes.

Terrified survivors on the icey cold ocean watched in horror as hundreds of fellow passengers went to their watery graves.

Captain Arthur Henry Rostron, captain of the Carpathia, supervised the rescue of 705 survivors.

Captain Rostron of the Cunard Steamship Line "Carpathia," heard the distress call and rushed his ship to aid the "Titanic" and take survivors aboard from the lifeboats. She was the only ship to come to the Titanic's rescue.

98

This photo, taken by a passenger aboard Carpathia shows Mr. and Mrs. Harder. They were newlyweds when the call went out to climb in the lifeboats. They believed there was no real danger and, on a lark, I jumped in the first lifeboat that was lowered.

The Titanic and Olympic on the stocks in Belfast.

These huge brackets held the gigantic screws in place on the Titanic.

There were 29 boilers that produced the power on the Titanic. They crashed through the bottom of the ship as she broke apart.

The Cunard Pier in New York awaiting the Carpathia to deliver survivors.

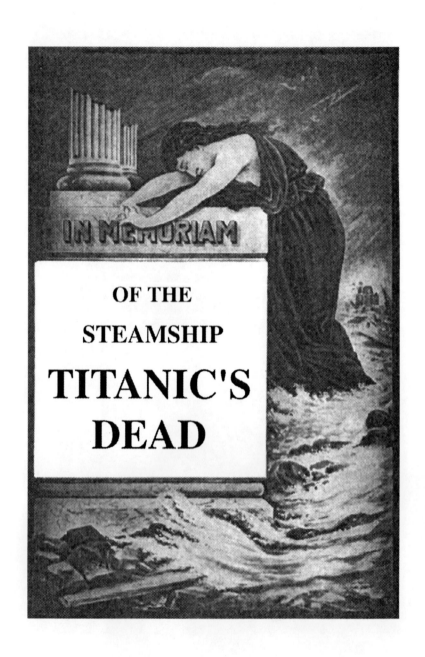

IN MEMORIAM

OF THE

STEAMSHIP

TITANIC'S
DEAD

30 Years of Survivor's Interviews & Clippings

*Grandma Anna (center) with
(left to right) George Thomas, Sam Thomas and
Dr. Joseph W. Thomas in the early 1970s*

Titanic survivor, George Thomas

Flint-Area Man, Mother Among Survivors of the Titanic

A Flint-area man and his mother have a special interest in today's observance of the 50th anniversary of the sinking of the Titanic, for they were among the 700 who survived.

They are George Thomas. 54, G-4040 H. Atherton Rd, and his mother, Mrs. Anna Thomas, 74, who lived in this area for many years but now is staying with another son. Sam, in North Hollywood, Calif.

Thomas, who operates a real-eatate business from his home, has lived in this area since 1926. He formerly owned two groceries here.

Thomas has no recollection of the tragedy. He was 4 years old at the time.

But through the years, his mother has told him how she,
I George and his late sister, Mary, were among the few who escaped.

The three were on their way to
America to join their husband sod father, Darwin, at Dowagiac, where he had a farm. They left Beirut, Lebanon, by ship for Marseilles, France. From there, they took a train to Paris and then to Cherbourg.

A smaller ship took them out to the Titanic, Thomas said.

"Mother wind to tell us how Mary, then 6, had gotten lost on the ship this particular night," Thomas said. "They looked all around and cüuldn't find her.

Mother told us she felt the ship strike something and then, after being pushed back slightly, strike it again. She opened the cabin door and heard someone yell that the ship had hit in iceberg.

"Many women just stayed in their cabins and prayed," Thomas said his mother told hint "Mother prayed too, but she also did something about it."

His mother grabbed bins and went to the ship's deck. For Some reason, she believed she would-need her purse, so she returned to the cabin. Near the cabin, she found Mary, who, it turned out, had fallen asleep in the cabin next door.

She snatched up the girl and returned to the deck where she had left her son.

"Mother told me that sailors put us in a lifeboat which was lowered to the water," Thomas went on. "She said that only another woman and her daughter were in the lifeboat, along With many sailors.

"Mother remembers seeing the lights of the ship. We were she

Mrs. Anna Thomas

heard a lot of noise and a safe distance away. Suddenly then the lights were gone, she said."

It is unknown how long they were in the lifeboat, Thomas said, but he believes it was a few hours.

Finally, they were picked up by the Csrpathia by means of a rope-and-bag system. Alter they reached New York, *they* immediately headed for Dowagiac and a husband and father who had received newa they were dead.

"I've thanked the Lord a million times since for what happened," Thomas said.then the lights were gone, she said."

108

Mrs. Anna Thomas

Rites slated Friday
for Anna Thomas

A Rosary will be recited at 8p.m. Thursday at Brown Funeral Home, 1616 Davison. Burial will be at New Calvary Cemetery. Flint Twp. She died Monday in Genesee Memorial Hospital.

Mrs. Thomas, a native of Beirut, Lebanon, was born in 1885. Mrs. Thomas and two children, George and Mary, were among only 700 survivors of the ill-fated Titanic, which sank in 1912. Mrs. Thomas and the children escaped by lifeboat. They later joined her husband, Darwin, who was living in Dowagiac.Mrs. Thomas also leaves two other sans, Joseph, Texas, and Samuel, California; 15 grandchildren, and 26 great-grandchildren.

June 28,1976

109

George Thomas says he was 8 years old when the Titanic sank in the Atlantic. He said he was not frightened, but his mother was. "Mother was putting the life jackets on us. She cried all the time."

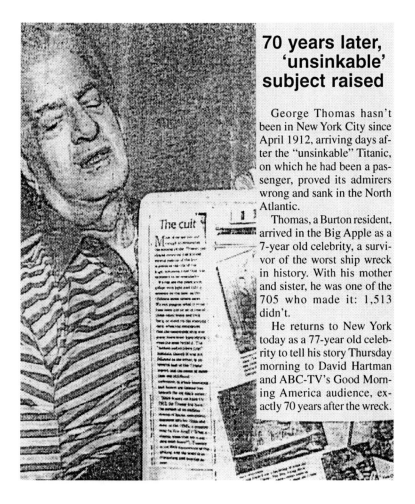

70 years later, 'unsinkable' subject raised

George Thomas hasn't been in New York City since April 1912, arriving days after the "unsinkable" Titanic, on which he had been a passenger, proved its admirers wrong and sank in the North Atlantic.

Thomas, a Burton resident, arrived in the Big Apple as a 7-year old celebrity, a survivor of the worst ship wreck in history. With his mother and sister, he was one of the 705 who made it: 1,513 didn't.

He returns to New York today as a 77-year old celebrity to tell his story Thursday morning to David Hartman and ABC-TV's Good Morning America audience, exactly 70 years after the wreck.

TITANIC SURVIVOR George Thomas,

Titanic survivor uneasy about disturbing grave

111

70 years later, 'unsinkable' subject raised

By MICHAEL ARKUSH
Journal staff writer

GeorgeThomas

George Thomas hasn't been in New York City since April 1912, arriving days after the "unsinkable" Titanic, on which he had been a passenger, proved its admirers wrong and sank in the North Atlantic.

GeorgeThomas, arrived in the Big Apple as a 8-year old celebrity, a survivor of the worst ship wreck in history. With his mother and sister, he was one of the 705 who made it: 1,513 didn't.

He returns to New York today as a 77-year old celebrity to tell his story Thursday morning to David Hartman and ABC-TV's Good Morning America audience, exactly 70 years after the wreck.

BURTON MAN FEATURED AS SURVIVOR OF THE TITANIC IN DOCUMENTARY

They said it was 'unsinkable' but as George Thomas of Burton knows, it was very sinkable. He should know, as he was he was one of the fortunate survivors from that "night to remember" when the glistening new British White Star Royal Mail Ship, the RMS Titanic sunk 2 1/2 miles into the depths of the North Atlantic ocean.

At the time. George (7-years old), his sister. Mary (9-years old) and his mother were on their way to discover America and join their father and husband, who had emigrated ahead of them from Lebanon and purchased a farm in Dowagiac, Michigan. As recounted in a recent interview with Laura Stevens, channel 28 Development assistant, Mr. Thomas recalls with exact clarity the events of that harrowing experience. His story is loaded with ironic twists of fate— from his family being that last to board the life boat to being the first to be rescued by the ship Carpathia—to being placed in the rescue boat by the Titanic's Captain, Edward J. Smith. Included in his story is the memory of his sister disappearance before the Titanic hit the iceberg and of his mother's discovery of his sister during a last minute check for valuables in their cabin. However, against incredible odds, Mr. Thomas, his sister and mother all eventually made it safely to Dowagiac.

Since the sinking of the Titanic in 1912, several theories and inquiries have been held re-

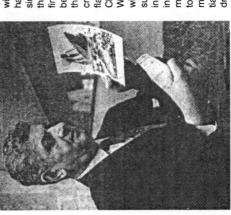

garding the cause for the tragedy. Last year five survivors, including Mr. Thomas, gathered in New York and Philadelphia to answer questions from the media, appear on the set of "Good Morning America," and relive their experience for award-winning British journalist Peter Williams. Williams has long been searching for the truth behind the sinking, uncovering new facts and discarding old theories. Among his discoveries has been the finding of the original Titanic model which has been hidden for 50 years and the revelation of the identity of the anonymous architect who secretly alerted the press to the Titanic's design flaws. In *Titanic: A Question of Murder*, to air on Channel 28 Wednesday, February 16 at 8 p.m., Williams presents his findings and theories along with the candid conversations of the remaining survivors who had gathered to share a harrowing and vivid 70-year old memory. Mr. Thomas is included in the taped coverage, however, for the most part he prefers to leave the speculation up to the authorities and public. This one-hour documentary will allow viewers the opportunity to partially experience the sinking of the Titanic and draw their own conclusions about the truth behind that "night to remember."

113

TITANIC MEMORY

GEORGE THOMAS *has become more interested in the history of the Titanic recently, even more so than being inducted as an honorary member of the Titanic Historical Society. He has newspapers dating from April, 1912, photos of the ship, and books telling about it.*

YEARS AFTER *the Titanic disaster, George Thomas found copies of newpapers detailing the accident and bought them. Thomas, his mother and sister were among the 705 survivors of the Titanic. The Titanic Historical Society estimates that there are approximately 30 survivors still living.*

Miscellaneous News

Titanic pass fetches $100,000 at auction

TACOMA. Wash. – An $8 Titanic boarding pass that survived the ill-fated voyage along with its passenger has fetched S 100,000 at an auction.

'the buyer was Jeffrey Trainer, an Allentown, Pa., collector who is in the trading-card business.

The price began at 55,000 on Saturday and zoomed to $100,000 in less than a minute, said Cheryl Gorsuch, co-owner of the Tacoma antique store where the auction was held,

Trainer said he would "hoard the ticket for a little while and enjoy it." The passenger, Anna Sofia Sjoblom. had "kept it for a while, so I may, too," he said.

The document–an undamagcd immigrant inspection card that served as a boarding pass for Titanic's third-class passcngers–is believed to be the only such ticket in existence. Its price Saturday makes it among the most valued of the ship's memorabilia.

Titanic sank on Sjoblom'a 18th birthday. She made it onto a lifeboat with the pass pinned inside her jacket.

Titanic memento nets $24,000 on auction block

LONDON – A postcard from the doomed Titanic, never mailed by the teenage passenger who wrote it, sold for more than $24,000 at an auction Friday.

Second-class passenger Edith Brown wrote the card to her step-sister in South Africa but still had it in her pocket when she jumped from the sinking ocean liner into a lifeboat in the early hours of April 15, 1912.

Thc buyer was Thomas Rogers, the owner of a shipping services company in Belfast, Northern Ireland, where the Titanic was built, Sotheby's auction house said Rogers paid $24,150 because he thought the postcard should he brought home.

116

Titanic survivor dies at 92

Last known male on board liner that sank in 1912

PARIS—Michel Navratil, one of the last known survivors of the sinking of the Titanic, has died in southern France. He was 92.

Navratil, who was 3 when the Titanic sank after striking an iceberg in 1912, died Wednesday in Montpellier. He was 'the last known male survivor, according to the Titanic Historical Society in Springfield, Mass.

'There are only four women left now," said Edward Kamuda, the society's founder.

Navratil and his 2-year-old brother, Edmond, were traveling with their father, who was separated from his wife and had taken his sons on the voyage without her permission.

Navratil described what happened when the ship began to sink:

"My father entered our cabin where we were sleeping. He dressed me very warmly and took me in his arms. A stranger did the same for my brother. When I think of it now, 1 am very moved. They knew they were going to die.

"I don't recall being afraid. I remember the pleasure really, of going plop into the lifeboat."

Navratil and his brother were rescued by the Car-patina, the first ship to reach the scene after racing through waters filled with icebergs. Navratil was hauled up the side of the Ship in a mail sack.

His father went down with the ship. Of the 2,228 people on board, only 705 survived.

When the boys reached the United States, they were taken in by a woman who met them aboard the ship. Their mother learned of their survival by reading newspaper reports about the boys, nicknamed "The Orphans of the Titanic" because no adult came forward to claim them.

Titanic Passenger List

This is the White Star Line's final passenger list of lost and saved, dated May 9, 1912. Those who were saved are in bold face type.

FIRST CLASS PASSENGERS

Allen, Miss Elizabeth Walton
Allison, Mr. H. J.
Allison, Mrs. H. J.
    and **Maid**
Allison, Miss L
Allison, Master T.
    and Nurse
Anderson, Mr. Harry
Andrews, Miss Cornelia I.
Andrews, Mr. Thomas
Appleton, Mrs. E. D.
Artagaveytia, Mr. Ramon
Astor, Colonel J. J.
    and Manservant
Astor, Mrs. J. J and Maid
Aubert, Mrs. N. and Maid
Barkworth, Mr. A. H.
Baumann, Mr. J.
Baxter, Mrs. James
Baxter, Mr. Quigg
Beattie, Mr. T.
Beckwith, Mr. R. L.
Beckwith, Mrs. R. L.
Behr, Mr. K. H.
Bishop, Mr. D. H.
Bishop, Mrs. D. H.
Bjornstrom, Mr. H.
Blackwell, Mr. Stephen Weart
Blank, Mr. Henry

Bonnell, Miss Caroline
Bonnell, Miss Lily
Borebank, Mr. J. J.
Bowen, Miss
Bowerman, Miss Elsie
Brady, Mr. John B.
Brandeis, Mr. E.
Brayton, Mr. George
Brewe, Dr Arthur Jackson
Brown, Mrs. J. J.
Brown, Mrs. J. M.
Bucknell, Mrs. W.
    and Maid
Butt, Major Archibald W.
Calderhead, Mr. E. P.
Candee, Mrs. Churchill
Cardoza, Mrs. J. W. M.
    and Maid
Cardoza, Mr. T. D. M
    and Manservant
Carlson, Mr. Frank
Carran, Mr. F. M.
Carran, Mr. J. P.
Carter, Mr. William E.
Carter, Mrs. William E.
    and Maid
Carter, Miss Lucile
Carter, Master William T.
    and Manservant

Case, Mr. Howard B.

Cassebeer, Mrs. H. A.

Cavendish, Mr. T.W.

**Cavendish, Mrs. T. W.
and Maid**

Chaffee, Mr. Herbert F.

Chaffee, Mrs. Herbert F.

Chambers, Mr. N. C.

Chambers, Mrs. N. C.

Cherry, Miss Gladys

Chevre, Mr. Paul

**Chibnafl, Mrs. E. M.
Bowerman**

Chisholm, Mr. Robert

Clark, Mr. Walter M.

Clark, Mrs. Walter M.

Clifford, Mr. George Quincy

Colley, Mr. E. P.

Compton, Mrs. A. T.

Compton, Miss S. P.

Compton, Mr. A. T., Jr.

Cornell, Mrs. R. G.

Crafton, Mr. John B.

Crosby, Mr. Edward G.

Crosby, Mrs. Edward G.

Crosby, Miss Harriet

Cummings, Mr. John Bradley

**Cummings, Mrs. John
Bradley**

Daly, Mr. P. D.

Daniel, Mr. Robert W.

Davidson, Mr. Thornton

Davidson, Mrs. Thornton

de Villiers, Mrs. B.

Dick, Mr. A. A.

Dick, Mrs. A. A.

Dodge, Dr. Washington

Dodge, Mrs. Washington

Dodge, Master Washington

Douglas, Mrs. F. C.

Douglas, Mr. W. D.

Douglas, Mrs. W. D.
and Maid

Dulles, Mr. William C.

Earnshew, Mrs. Boulton

Endres, Miss Caroline

Eustis, Miss E. M.

Evans, Miss E.

Flegenheim, Mrs. A.

Flynn, Mr. J. I.

Foreman, Mr. B. L.

Fortune, Mr. Mark

Fortune, Mrs. Mark

Fortune, Miss Ethel

Fortune, Miss Alice

Fortune, Miss Mabel

Fortune, Mr. Charles

Franklin, Mr. T. P.

Frauenthal Mr. T. G.

Frauenthal, Dr. Henry W.

Frauenthal, Mrs. Henry W.

Frolicher, Miss Marguerite

Futrelle, Mr. J.

Futrelle, Mrs. J.

Gee, Mr. Arthur

Gibson, Mrs. L..

Gibson, Miss D.

Giglio, Mr. Victor

Goldenberg, Mr. S. L.

Goldenberg, Mrs. S. L.

Goldschmidt, Mrs. George B.

Gordon, Sir Cosmo Duff

Gordon, Lady Duff and Maid

Gracie, Colonel Archibald

Graham, Mr.

Graham, Mrs William G

Graham, Miss Margaret

Greenfield, Mrs. L. D.

Greenfield, Mrs. W. B.

Guggenheim, Mr Benjamin

Harder, Mr. George A.

Harder, Mrs. George A.

**Harper, Mr. Henry Sleeper
     and Manservant**

Harper, Mrs. Henry Sleeper

Harris, Mr. Henry B.

Harris, Mrs. Henry B.

Harrison, Mr. W. H.

Haven, Mr. H.

Hawksford, Mr. W. J.

Hays, Mr. Charles M.

Hays, Mrs. Charles M.
     and Maid

**Hays, Miss Margaret Head,
Mr. Christopher**

Hilliard, Mr. Herbert Henry

Hipkins, Mr. W. E.

Hippach, Mrs. Ida S.

Hippach, Miss Jean

Hogeboom, Mrs. John C.

Holverson, Mr. A. O.

Holverson, Mrs. A. O.

Hoyt, Mr. Frederick M.

Hoyt, Mrs. Frederick M.

Holt, Mr. W. F.

Isham, Mrs. A. E.

Ismay, Mr. J. Bruce
     and Manservant

Jakob, Mr. Birnbaum

Jones, Mr. C. C

Julian, Mr. H. F.

Kent, Mr. Edward A.

Kenyon, Mr. F. R.

Kenyon, Mrs. F. R.

Kimball, Mr. E. N.

Kimball, Mrs. E. N.

Klaber, Mr. Herman

Lambert-Williams, Mr.

Fletcher Fellows

Leader, Mrs. F. A.

Lewy, Mr. E. G.

Lindstroem, Mrs. J.

Lines, Mrs. Ernest H.

Lines, Miss Mary C.

Lingrey Mr Edward

Long, Mr.. Milton C.

Langley, Miss Gretchen F.

Loring, Mr. J. H.

**Madill, Miss Georgette
Alexandra**

Maguire, Mr. J. E.

Marechal, Mr. Pierre

Marvin, Mr. D. W.

Marvin, Mrs. D. W.

McCaffry. Mr. T.

McCarthy, Mr. Timothy J.

McGough, Mr. J. R.

Meyer, Mr. Edgar J.

Meyer, Mrs. Edgar J.

Millet, Mr. Frank D.

Missahan, Dr. W. E.

Missahan, Mrs. W. B.

Missahan, Miss Daisy

Moch, Mr. Pkdtp E.

122

Moch, Mr. Phillip E.

Molson, Mr. H. Markland

Moore, Mr. Clarence
and Manservant

Natsch, Mr. Charles

Newell, Mr. A. W.

Newell, Miss Alice

Newell, Miss Madeline

Newsom, Miss Helen

Nicholson, Mr. A. S.

Omont, Mr. F.

Ostby, Mr. E. C

Ostby, Miss Helen R.

Ovies, Mr. S.

Parr, Mr. M. H. W.

Partner, Mr. Austin

Payne, Mr. V.

Pears, Mr. Thomas

Pears, Mrs. Thomas

Penasco, Mr. Victor

Penasco, Mrs. Victor and Maid

Peuchen, Major Arthur

Porter, Mr. Walter Chamberlain

Potter, Mrs. Thomas, Jr.

Reuchlin, Mr. Jonkheer, J. G.

Rheims, Mr. George

**Robert, Mrs. Edward S.
and Maid**

Roebling, Mr. Washington A. 2nd

Rolmane, Mr. C.

Rood, Mr. Hugh R.

Rosenbaum, Miss

Ross, Mr. J. Hugo

**Rothes, the Countess of
and Maid**

Rothschild, Mr. M.

Rothschild, Mrs. M.

Rowe, Mr. Alfred

Ryerson, Mr. Arthur

**Ryerson, Mrs. Arthur
and Maid**

Ryerson, Miss Emily

Ryerson, Miss Susan

Ryerson, Master Jack

Saalfeld, Mr. Adolphe

Schabert, Mrs. Paul

Seward, Mr. Frederick K.

Shutes, Miss E. W.

Silverthorne, Mr. S. V.

Silvey, Mr. William B.

Silvey, Mrs. William B.

Simonius, Mr. Oberst Altons

Sloper, Mr. William T.

Smart, Mr. John M.

Smith, Mr. J. Clinch

Smith, Mr. R. W.

Smith, Mr. L P.

Smith, Mrs. L P.

Snyder, Mr. John

Snyder, Mrs. John

Soloman, Mr. A. L.

Spedden, Mr. Frederick O.

**Spedden, Mrs. Frederick O.
and Maid**

**Spedden, Master R. Douglas
and Nurse**

Spencer, Mr. W. A.

Spencer, Mrs. W. A.
and Maid

Stahelin, Dr. Max

Stead, Mr. W. T.

Steffanson, B. B.

123

Steffanon, H. B.
Stehli, Mr. Max Frolicher
Stehli, Mrs. Max Frolicher
Stengel, Mr. C. E. H.
Stengel, Mrs. C. E. H.
Stewart, Mr. A. A.
Stone, Mrs. George M.
    and Maid
Straus, Mr. Isidor
    and Manservant
Straus, Mrs. Isidor and **Maid**
Sutton, Mr. Frederick
Swift, Mrs. Frederick Joel
Taussig, Mr. Emil
Taussig, Mrs. Emil
Taussig, Miss Ruth
Taylor, Mr. E. Z
Taylor, Mrs. E. Z.
Thayer, Mr. J. B.
Thayer, Mrs. J. B.
    and Maid
Thayer, Mr. J. B., Jr.
Thorne, Mr. G.
Thorne, Mrs. G.
Tucker, Mr. G. M., Jr.
Uruchurtu, Mr. M. R.
Van der Hoef, Mr. Wyckoff
Walker, Mr. W. Anderson
Warren, Mr. F. M.
Warren, Mrs. F. M.
Weir, Mr. J.
White, Mr. Percival W.
White, Mr. Richard F.
White, Mrs. J. Stuart
    Maid & Manservant
Wick, Mr. George D.

Wick, Mrs. George D.
Wick, Miss Mary
Widener, Mr. George D.
    and Manservant
Widener, Mrs. George D.
    and Maid
Widener, Mr.. Harry
Willard, Miss Constance
Williams, Mr. Duane
Williams, Mr. R. N., Jr.
Woolner, Mr. Hugh
Wright, Mr. George
Young, Miss Marie

SECOND CLASS PASSENGERS

Abelson, Mr. Samson
Abelson, Mrs. Hanna
Aldworth, Mr. C.
Andrew, Mr. Edgar
Andrew, Mr. Frank
Angle, Mr. William
Angle, Mrs.
Ashby, Mr. John
Baily, Mr. Percy
Baimbridge, Mr. Chas. R.
Balls, Mrs. Ada E.
Banfield, Mr. Frederick J.
Bateman, Mr. Robert J.
Beane, Mr. Edward
Beane, Mrs. Ethel
Beauchamp, Mr. H. J.
Becker, Mrs. A. O.
    and 3 children
Beesley, Mr. Lawrence
Bentham, Miss Lilian W.

Berriman, Mr. William

Botsford, Mr. W. Hull

Bowenur, Mr. Solomon

Bracken, Mr. Jas. H.

Brito, Mr. Jose de

Brown, Miss Mildred

Brown, Mr. S.

Brown, Mrs.

Brown, Miss E.

Bryhl, Mr. Curt

Bryhl, Miss Dagmar

Buss, Miss Kate

Butler, Mr. Reginald

Byles, Rev.nomas R. D.

Bystrom, Miss Karolina

Caldwell, Mr. Albert F.

Caldwell, Mrs. Sylvia

Caldwell, Master Alden G.

Cameron, Miss Clear

Carbines, Mr. William

Carter, Rev. Ernest C.

Carter, Mrs. Lillian

Chapman, Mr. John H.

Chapman, Mrs. Elizabeth

Chapman, Mr. Charles

Christy, Mrs. Alice

Christy, Miss Juli

Clarke, Mr. Charles V.

Clarke, Mrs. Ada Maria

Coleridge, Mr. R. C.

Collander, Mr. Erik

Collett, Mr. Stuart

Collyer, Mr. Harvey

Collyer, Mrs. Charlotte

Collyer, Miss Marjorie

Corbett, Mrs. Irene

Corey, Mrs. C. P.

Cotterill, Mr. Harry

Davies, Mr. Charles

Davis, Mrs. Agnes

Davis, Master John M.

Davis, Miss Mary

Deacon, Mr. Percy

del Carlo, Mr. Sebastian

del Carlo, Mrs.

Denbou, Mr. Herbert

Dibden, Mr. William

Doling, Mrs. Ada

Doling, Miss Elsie

Downton, Mr. William J.

Drachstedt, Baron von

Drew, Mr. James V.

Drew, Mrs. Lulu

Drew, Master Marshall

Duran, Miss Florentina

Duran, Miss Asimcion

Eitemiller, Mr. G. F.

Enander, Mr. Ingvar

Fahlstrom Mr. Arne J.

Faunthorpe, Mr. Harry

Faunthorpe, Mrs. Lizzie

Fillbrook, Mr. Charles

Fox, Mr. Stanley H.

Funk, Miss Annie

Fynney, Mr. Jos.

Gale, Mr. Harry

Gale, Mr. Shadrach

Garside, Miss Ethel

Gaskell, Mr. Alfred

Gavey, Mr. Lawrence

Gilbert, Mr. William

Giles, Mr. Edgar

Giles, Mr. Fred
Giles, Mr. Ralph
Gill, Mr. John
Gillespie, Mr. William
Givard, Mr. Hans K.
Greenberg, Mr. Samuel
Hale, Mr. Reginald
Hamalainer, Mrs. Anna
    and Infant
Harbeck, Mr. Wm. H.
Harper, Mr. John
Harper, Miss Nina
Harris, Mr. George
Harris, Mr. Walter
Hart, Mr. Benjamin
Hart, Mrs. Esther
Hart, Miss Eva
Herman, Miss Alice
Herman, Mrs. Jane
Herman, Miss Kate
Herman, Mr. Samuel
Hewlett, Mrs. Mary D.
Hickman, Mr. Leonard
Hickman, Mr. Lewis
Hickman, Mr. Stanley
Hiltunen, Miss Martha
Hocking, Mr. George
Hocking, Mrs. Elizabeth
Hocking, Miss Nellie
Hocking, Mr. Samuel J.
Hodges, Mr. Henry P.
Hoffman, Mr. and **2 children:**
    (Loto & Louis)
Hold, Mrs. Annie
Hold, Mr. Stephen
Hood, Mr. Ambrose

Hosono, Mr. Masabumi
Howard, Mr. Benjamin
Howard, Mrs. Ellen T.
Hunt, Mr. George
Ilett, Miss Bertha
Jacobsohn, Mrs. Amy P.
Jacobsohn Mr. Sidney S.
Jarvis, Mr. John D.
Jefferys, Mr. Clifford
Jefferys, Mr. Ernest
Jenkin, Mr. Stephen
Jervan, Mrs. A. T.
Kantor, Mrs. Miriam
Kantor, Mr. Sehua
Karnes, Mrs. J. F.
Keane, Mr. Daniel
Keane, Miss Nora A.
Kelly, Mrs. F.
Kirkland, Rev. Charles L
Kvillner, Mr. John Henrik
Lahtinen, Mrs. Anna
Lahtinen, Mr. William
Lamb, Mr. J. J.
Lamore, Mrs. Ameliar
Laroche, Mr. Joseph
Laroche, Mrs. Juliet
Laroche, Miss Louise
Laroche, Miss Simonne
Lehman, Miss Bertha
Leitch, Miss Jessie
Levy, Mr. R. J.
Leyson, Mr. Robert W. N.
Lingan, Mr. John
Louch, Mr. Charles
Louch, Mrs. Alice Adela
Mack, Mrs. Mary

126

Malachard, Mr. Noel
Mallet, Mr. A.
Mallet, Mrs.
Mallet, Master A.
Mangiavacchi, Mr. Emilio
Mantvila, Mr. Joseph
Marshall, Mr.
Marshall, Mrs. Kate
Matthews, Mr. W. J.
Maybery, Mr. Frank H.
McCrae, Mr. Arthur G.
McCrie, Mr. James
McKane, Mr. Peter D.
Mellers, Mr. William
Mellinger, Mrs. Elizabeth
and Child
Meyer, Mr. August
Milling, Mr. Jacob C.
Mitchell, Mr. Henry
Morawick, Dr. Ernest
Mudd, Mr. Thomas C.
Myles, Mr. Thomas F.
Nasser, Mr. Nicolas
Nasser, Mrs.
Nesson, Mr. Israel
Nicholls, Mr. Joseph C.
Norman, Mr. Robert D.
Nye, Mrs. Elizabeth
Otter, Mr. Richard
Oxenham, Mr. P. Thomas
Padro, Mr. Julian
Pain, Dr. Alfred
Pallas, Mr. Emilio
Parker, Mr. Clifford R.
Parrish, Mrs. L Davis
Pengelly, Mr. Frederick

Pernot, Mr. Rene
Peruschitz, Rev. Jos. M.
Phillips, Mr. Robert
Phillips, Miss Alice
Pinsky, Miss Rosa
Ponesell, Mr. Martin
Portaluppi, Mr. Emilio
Pulbaun, Mr. Frank
Quick, Mrs. Jane
Quick, Miss Vera W.
Quick, Miss Phyllis
Reeves, Mr. David
Renouf, Mr. Peter H.
Renouf, Miss Lillie
Reynolds, Miss E.
Richard, Mr. Emile
Richards, Mrs. Emily
Richards, Master William
Richards, Master George
Ridsdale, Miss Lucy
Rogers, Mr. Harry
Rogers, Miss Selina
Rugg, Miss Emily
Sedgwick, Mr. C. F. W.
Sharp, Mr. Percival
Shelley, Mrs. Imanita
Silven, Miss Lyyli
Sincook, Miss Maude
Sinkkenen, Miss Anna
Sjostedt, Mr. Ernest A.
Slayter, Miss H. M.
Slemen, Mr. Richard J.
Smith, Mr. Augustus
Smith, Miss Marion
Sobey, Mr. Hayden
Stanton, Mr. S. Ward

Stokes, Mr. Phillip J.
Swane, Mr. George
Sweet, Mr. George
Toomey, Miss Ellen
Trant, Miss Jessie
Tronpiansky, Mr. Moses A.
Troutt, Miss E. Celia
Tupin, M. Dorothy
Turpin, Mr. William J.
Veale, Mr. James
Walcroft, Miss Nellie
Ware, Mrs. Florence L
Ware, Mr. John James
Ware, Mr. William J.
Watt, Miss Bertha
Watt, Mrs. Bessie
Webber, Miss Susie
Weisz, Mr. Leopold
Weisz, Mrs. Matilda
Wells, Mrs. Addie
Wells, Miss J.
Wells, Master Ralph
West, Mr. E. Arthur
West, Mrs. Ada
West, Miss Barbara
West, Miss Constance
Wheadon, Mr. Edward
Wheeler, Mr. Edwin

THIRD CLASS
PASSENGERS
British subjects embarked at
Southampton.
Abbott, Eugene
Abbott, Rosa
Abbott, Rossmore

Abbing, Anthony
Adams. J.
Aks, Filly
Aks, Leah
Alexander, William
Allen, William
Allum, Owen G.
Badman, Emily
Barton David
Beavan, W. T.
Billiard, A. van
Billiard, James (child)
Billiard, Walter (child)
Bing, Lee
Bowen, David
Braund, Lewis
Braund, Owen
Brocklebank, William
Cann, Erenst
Carver, A.
Celotti, Francesco
Chip, Chang
Christmann, Emil
Cohen, Gurshon
Cook, Jacob
Corn, Harry
Coutts, Winnie
Coutts, William (child)
Coutts, Leslie (child)
Coxon, Daniel
Crease, Ernest James
Cribb, John Hatfield
Cribb, Alice
Dahl, Charles
Davies, Evan
Davies, Alfred

Davies, John
Davies, Joseph
Davison, Thomas H.
Davison, Mary
Dean, Mr. Bertram F.
Dean, Mrs. Hetty
Dean, Bertran (child)
Dean, Vera (infant)
Dennis, Samuel
Dennis, William
Derkings, Edward
Dowdell, Elizabeth
Drapkin, Jenie
Dugemin, Joseph
Elsbury, James
Emanuel, Ethet (child)
Everett, Thomas J.
Foo, Choong
Ford, Arthur
Ford, Margaret
Ford, Mrs. D. M.
Ford, Mr. E. W.
Ford, M. W. T. N.
Ford, Maggie (child)
Franklin, Charles
Garthfirth, John
Gilinski, Leslie
Godwin, Frederick
Goldsmith, Frank J.
Goldsmith, Emily A.
Goldsmith, Frank J. W.
Goodwin, Augusta
Goodwin, Lillian A.
Goodwin, Charles E.
Goodwin, William F. (child)
Goodwin, Jessie (child)

Goodwin, Harold (child)
Goodwin, Sidney (child)
Green, George
Guest, Robert
Harknett, Alice
Harmer, Abraham
Hee, Ling
Howard, May
Hyman, Abraham
Johnston, A. G.
Johnston, Mrs.
Johnston, William (child)
Johnston, Mrs. C. H. (child)
Johnson, Mr. A.
Johnson, Mr. W.
Keefe, Arthur
Kelly, James
Lam, Ali
Lam, Len
Lang, Fang
Leonard, Mr. L
Lester, J.
Ling, Lee
Lithman, Simon
Lobb, Cordelia
Lobb, William A.
Lockyer, Edward
Lovell, John
MacKay, George W.
Maisner, Simon
McNamee, Eileen
McNamee, Neal
Meanwell, Marian O.
Meek, Annie L.
Meo, Alfonso
Miles, Frank

Moor, Beile
Moor, Meier
Moore, Leonard C.
Morley, William
Moutal, Rahamin
Murdlin, Joseph
Nancarrow, W. H.
Niklasen, Sander
Nosworthy, Richard C.
Peacock, Alfred
Peacodc., Treasteall
Peacock, Treasteall (child)
Pearce, Ernest
Peduzzi, Joseph
Perkin, John Henry
Peterson, Marius
Potchett, George
Rath, Sarah
Reed, James George
Reynolds, Harold
Risien, Emma
Risien, Samuel
Robins, Alexander
Robins, Charity
Rogers, William John
Rouse, Richard H.
Rush, Alfred George J.
Sadowitz, Harry
Sage, John
Sage, Annie
Sage, Stella
Sage, George
Sage, Douglas
Sage, Frederick
Sage, Dorothy
Sage, William (child)

Sage, Ada (child)
Sage, Constance (child)
Sage, Thomas (child)
Sather, Sinon
Saundercock, W. H.
Sawyer, Frederick
Scrota, Maurice
Shellard, Frederick
Shorney, Charles
Simmons, John
Slocovski, Selman
Somerton, Francis W.
Spector, Woolf
Spinner, Henry
Stanley, Amy
Stanley, E. R. Mr.
Storey, T. Mr.
Sunderland, Victor
Sutehall, Henry
Theobald, Thomas
Thomas, Alex
Thorneycrolt, Florence
Thorneycroft, Percival
Tomlin, Ernest P.
Torber, Ernest
Trembisky, Berk
Tunquist, W.
Ware, Frederick
Warren, Charles W.
Webber, James
Wilkes, Ellen
Willey, Edward
Williams, Harry
Williams, Leslie
Windelov, Einar
Wiseman, Philip

Foreigners embarked at Southampton.

Abelseth, Karen
Abelseth, Olaus
Abramson, August
Adahl, Mauritz
Adolf, Humblin
Ahlin, Johanna
Ahmed, Ali
Alhomaki, Ilmari
Ali, William
Anderson, Alfreda
Anderson, Erna
Anderson, Albert
Anderson, Anders
Anderson, Samuel
Anderson, Sigrid (child)
Anderson, Thor
Anderson, Carla
Anderson, Ingeborg (child)
Anderson, Ebba (child)
Anderson, Sigvard (child)
Anderson, Ellis
Anderson, Ida Augusta
Anderson, Paul Edvin
Angheloff, Minko
Asplund, Carl (child)
Asplund, Charles
Aspland, Felix (child)
Asplund, Gustaf (child)
Asplund, Johan
Asplund, Lillian (child)
Asplund, Oscar (child)
Asplund, Selma
Arnold, Joseph
Arnold, Josephine
Aronsson, Ernest Axel A.
Asim, Adola
Assam, Ali
Augustsan, Albert
Backstrom, Karl
Backstrom, Marie

Balkic, Cerin
Benson, John Viktor
Berglund. Ivar
Berkeland, Hans
Bjorklund, Ernst
Bostandyeff, Guentcho
Braf, Elin Ester
Brobek, Carl R.
Cacic, Grego
Cacic, Luka
Cacic, Maria
Cacic, Manda
Calie, Peter
Carlson, Carl R.
Carlsson, Julius
Carlsson, August Sigfrid
Coelho, Domingos Fernardeo
Coleff, Fotio
Coleff, Peyo
Cor, Bartol
Cor, Ivan
Cor, Ludovik
Dahl, Mauritz
Dahlberg, Gerda
Dakic, Branko
Danbom, Ernest
Danbom, Gillber (infant)
Danoff, Sigrid
Danoff, Yoto
Dantchoff, Khristo
Delalic, Regyo
Denkoff, Mito
Dimic, Jovan
Dintcheff, Valtcho
Dyker, Adoff
Dyker, Elizabeth
Ecimovic, Joso
Edwardsson, Gustaf
Eklunz, Hans
Ekstrom, Johan
Finote, Luigi
Fischer, Eberhard

131

Goldsmith, Nathan
Goncalves, Manoel E.
Gronnestad, Daniel D.
Gustafson, Alfred
Gustafson, Anders
Gustafson, Johan
Gustafsson, Gideon
Haas, Aloisia
Hadman, Oscar
Hagland, Ingvald O.
Hagland, Konrad R.
Hakkurainen, Pekko
Hakkurainen, Elin
Hampe, Leon
Hankonen, Eluna
Hansen, Claus
Hansen, Janny
Hansen, Henry Damgavd
Heininen, Wendla
Hendekevoic, Ignaz
Henriksson, Jenny
Hervonen, Helga
Hervonen, Hildwe (child)
Hickkinen, Laina
Hillstrom, Hilda
Holm, John F. A.
Holten, Johan
Humblin, Adolf
Ilieff, Ylio
Ilmakangas, Ida
Ilmakangas, Pista
Ivanoff, Konio
Jansen, Carl
Jardin, Jose Netto
Jensen, Carl
Jensen, Hans Peter
Jensen, Svenst L.
Jensen, Nilho R.
Johannessen, Bernt
Johannessen, Elias
Johansen, Nils
Johanson, Oscar

Johanson, Oscal L.
Johansson, Erik
Johansson, Gustaf
Johnson, Jakob A.
Johnson, Alice
Johnson, Harold
Johnson, Eleanora (infant)
Johnsson, Carl
Johnsson, Malkolm
Jonkoff, Lazor
Jonsson, Nielo H.
Jusila, Katrina
Jusila, Mari
Jusila, Erik
Jutel, Henrik Hansen
Kallio, Nikolai
Kalvig Johannes H.
Karajic, Milan
Karlson, Einar
Karlson, Nils August
Kekic, Tido
Kink, Anton
Kink, Louise
Kink, Louise (child)
Kink, Maria
Kink, Vincenz
Klasen, Klas A.Mona, Mae A.
Klasen, Hilda
Klasen, Gertrud (child)
Laitinen, Sofia
Laleff, Kristo
Landegren, Aurora
Larson, Viktor
Larsson, Bengt Edvin
Larsson, Edvard
Lefebre, Frances
Lefebre, Henry (child)
Lefebre, Ida (child)
Lefebre, Ida (child)
Lefebre,Mathilde (child)
Leinonen, Antti
Lindablom, August

Lindell, Edvard B.
Lindell, Elin
Lindahl, Agda
Lindqvist, Einar
Lulic, Nicola
Lundahl, John
Lundin, Olga
Lundstripm, Jan
Madsen, Fridjof
Maenpaa, Matti
Makinen, Kalle
Mampe, Leon
Marinko, Dmitri
Markoff, Marin
Melkebuk, Philemon
Messemacker, Guillaume
Messemacker, Emma
Midtsjo, Carl
Mikanen, John
Misseff, Ivan
Minkoff, Lazar
Mirko, Dika
Mitkoff, Mito
Moen, Sigurd H.
Moss, Albert
Mulder, Theo
Myhrman, Oliver
Naidenoff, Penko
Nankoff, Minko
Nedeco, Petroff
Nenkoff, Christo
Nieminen, Manta
Nilsson, August F.
Nilson, Berta
Nilson, Helmina
Nirva, Isak
Nyoven, Johan
Nyston, Anna
Odahl, Martin
Orman, Velin
Olsen, Arthur
Olsen, Carl

Olsen, Henry
Olsen, Ole M.
Olson, Elon
Olsson, John
Olsson, Elida
Oreskovic, Luka
Oreskovic, Maria
Oreskovic, Jeko
Osman, Mara
Pacruic, Mate
Pacruic, Tome
Panula, Eino
Panula, Ernesti
Panula, Juho
Panula, Maria
Panula, Sanni
Panula, Urhu (child)
Panula, William (infant)
Pasic, Jakob
Pentcho, Petroff
Paulsson, Alma C
Paulsson, Gosta (child)
Paulsson, Paul (child)
Paulsson, Stina(child)
Paulsson, Torborg (child)
Pavlovic, Stefo
Pekonemi, E.
Pelsmaker, Alfons de
Peltomaki, Nikolai
Person, Ernest
Peterson, Johan
Peterson, Ellen
Petranec, Matilda
Petterson, Olaf
Plotcharsky, Vasil
Radeff, Alexander
Rintamaki, Matti
Rosblom, Helene
Rosblom, Salfi (child)
Rosblom, Viktor
Rummstvedt, Kristian
Salander, Carl

Saljilsvik, Anna
Salonen, Werner
Sandman, Johan
Sandstrom, Agnes
Sandstrom, Beatrice (child)
Sandstrom, Margretha (child)
Sdycoff, Todor
Sheerlinck, Jean
Sihvola, Antti
Sivic, Husen
Sjoblom, Anna
Skoog, Anna
Skoog, Carl (child)
Skoog, Harald (child)
Skoog, Mabel (child)
Skoog, Margret (child)
Skoog, William
Slabenoff, Petco
Smiljanic, Mile
Sohole, Peter
Solvang, Lena Jacobsen
Sop, Jules
Staneff, Ivan
Stoytcho, Mihoff
Stoyehoff, Ilia
Strandberg, Ida
Stranden, Jules
Strilic, Ivan
Strom, Selma (child)
Svensen, Olaf
Svensson, Johan
Svensson, Coverin
Syntakoff, Stanko
Tikkanen, Juho
Todoroff, Lalio
Tonglin, Gunner
Turcin, Stefan
Turgo, Anna
Twekula, Hedwig
Uzelas, Jovo
Waelens, Achille

Van Impe, Catharine (child)
Van Impe, Jacob
Van Impe, Rosalie
Van der Planke, Augusta
Vander
Van der Planke, Emilie Vander
Van der Planke, Jules Vander
Van der Planke, Leon Vander
Van der Steen, Leo
Van de Velde, Joseph
Van de Walle, Nestor
Vereruysse, Victor
Vook, Janko
Wende, Olof Edvin
Wennerstrom, August
Wenzel, Zinhart
Vestrom, Huld A. A.
Widegrin, Charles
Wiklund, Karl F.
Wiklund, Jacob A.
Wirz, Albert
Wittenrongel, Camille
Zievens, Renee
Zimmermann, Leo

Embarked at Cherbourg.
Assaf, Marian
Attala, Malake
Baclini, Latila
Baclini, Maria
Baclini, Eugene
Baclini, Helene
Badt, Mohamed
Banoura, Ayout
Barbara, Catherine
Barbara, Saude
Betros, Tannous
Boulos, Hanna
Boulos, Sultani
Boulos, Nourelain
Boulos, Akar (child)
Banous, Elias

Caram, Joseph
Caram, Maria
Shabini, Georges
Chehab, Emir Farres
Chronopoulos, Apostolos
Cbronopoulos, Demetrios
Dibo, Elias
Drazenovie, Josip
Elias, Joseph
Elias, Joseph
Fabini, Leeni
Fat-ma, Mustmani
Gerios, Assaf
Gerios, Youssef
Gerios, Youssef
Gheorgheff, Stanio
Hanna, Mansour
Jean Nassr, Saade
Johann, Markim
Joseph, Mary
Karun, Franz
Karun, Anna (child)
Kassan, M. Housseing
Kassem, Fared
Kassein, Hassef
Kalil, Betros
Khalil, Zahie
Kraeff, Thodor
Lemberopoulos, Peter
Malinoff, Nicola
Meme, Hanna
Monbarek, Hanna
Moncarek, Omine
Moncarek, Gonios (child)
Moncarek, Halim (child)
Moussa, Mantoura
Naked, Said
Naked, Waika
Naked, Maria
Nasr, Mustafa
Nichan, Krikorian
Nicola, Jamila

Nicola, Elias (child)
Novel, Mansouer
Orsen, Sirayanian
Ortin, Zakarian
Peter, Catherine Joseph
Peter, Mike
Peter, Anna
Rafoul, Baccos
Raibid, Razi
Saad, Amin
Saad, Khalil
Samaan, Hanna
Samaan, Elias
Samaan, Youssef
Sarkis, Mardirosian
Sarkis, Lahowd
Seman Betros (child)
Shedid, Daher
Sleiman, Attalla
Stankovic, Jovan
Tannous, Thomas
Tannous, Daler
Thomas, CharlesP
Thomas, Tamin
Thomas, Assad (infant)
Thomas, John
Tonfik, Nahli
Torfa, Assad
Useher,Baulner
Vagil, Adele Jane
Vartunian, David
Vassilios, Catavelas
Wazli, Yousif
Weller, Abi
Yalsevae, Ivan
Yazbeck, Antoni
Yazbeck, Salini
Youssef, Brahim
Youssef, Hanne
Youssef, Maria (child)
Youssef Georges (child)
Zabour. Tamini

Zabour, Hileni
Zakarian, Maprieder

Embarked at Queenstown.
Barry, Julia
Bourke, Catherine
Bourke, John
Bradley, Bridget
Buckley, Daniel
Buckley, Katherine
Burke, Jeremiak
Burke, Mary
Burns, Mary
Canavan, Mary
Carr, Ellen
Car, Jeannie
Chartens, David
Cannavan, Pat
Colbert, Patrick
Conlin, Thos. H.
Connaghton, Michel
Connors, Pat
Conolly, Kate
Conolly, Kate
Daly, Marcella
Daly, Eugene
Devanoy, Margaret
Dewan, Frank
Dooley, Patrick
Doyle, Elin
Driscoll, Bridget
Emmeth, Thomas
Farrell, James
Foley, Joseph
Foley, William
Flynn, James
McGowan, Annie
McMahon, Martin
Mechan, John
Meeklave, Ellie
Moran, James
Moran, Bertha

Morgan, Daniel J.
Morrow, Thomas
Mullens, Katie
Mulvihill, Bertha
Murphy, Norah
Murphy, Mary
Murphy, Kate
Naughton, Hannah
Nemagh, Robert
O'Brien, Denis
O'Brien, Thomas
O'Brien, Hannah
O'Connell, Pat D.
O'Connor, Maurice
O'Connor, Pat
O'Donaghue, Bert
O'Dwyer, Nellie
O'Keefe, Pat
OLeary, Norah
O'Neill, Bridget
O'Sullivan, Bridget
Peters, Katie
Rice, Margaret
Rice, Albert (child)
Rice, George (child)
Rice, Eric (child)
Rice, Arthur (child)
Rice, Eugene (child)
Riordan, Hannah
Ryan, Patrick
Ryan, Edw.
Sadlier, Matt
Scanlan, James
Shaughnesay, Pat
Shine, Ellen
Smyth, Julian
Tobin, Roger

Printed in the United States
58159LVS00005B/298-396

9 781425 921927